the

GW00640676

verbier
val de bagnes

first edition 2003

written and edited by
Isobel Rostron & Michael Kayson

winter press
www.snowmole.com

the snowmole guide to **verbier val de bagnes**
first edition 2003

published by winter press
45 Mysore Road London SW11 5RY

printed by Cambrian Printers
Llanbadarn Road Aberystwyth Ceredigion SY23 3TN

ISBN 0-9545739-0-0

A catalogue record of this book is available from the British Library.

contents

about snowmole

snowmole / snṓmōl / n. & v. **1** a spy operating within alpine territory (esp. ski resorts) for the purpose of gathering local knowledge. **2** (in full **snowmole guide**) the guidebook containing information so gathered. v. research or compile or process intelligence on an alpine resort or surrounding mountainous area.

the idea
How much you enjoy your winter holiday depends on a variety of things. Some you cannot influence - you can't guarantee sunshine, good snow, or your flight landing on time... but most things should be within your control. With the majority of ski holidays lasting just a week or less, you don't want to waste time trying to find a good restaurant, or struggling with an overgrown piste map. The snowmole guides are designed with two purposes in mind: to save you time by providing essential information on the operation of the resort, and to help you to make the most of your time by giving insight into every aspect of your stay.

how to use the guide
The guide is not intended to be read from cover to cover. It is split into four distinct sections, and some information will be useful to you beforehand, some while you are in resort, some while on the mountain.

getting started deals with the basics: how to get to the resort, how to get around once you're there, and your options when buying your lift pass, renting equipment and booking lessons or mountain guides.

the skiing gives an overview of the mountains and the ski areas, contains detailed descriptions of pistes and lifts as well as a section covering the off-piste, and a breakdown for beginners, intermediates, experts, boarders and non-skiers.

the resort covers the best of the rest of your holiday: a series of reviews on where to eat, where to play, where to stay and what to do when skiing isn't an option. Some reviews are extended as 'features', and everything is cross-referenced to either the valley or the town map.

the a-z comprises a directory of contact details and information, from accidents to weather, a glossary of terms used in this guide and in skiing in general, and an index to help navigate your way around the guide.

maps
The guide features maps designed and produced specifically for snowmole. While the information they contain is as accurate as possible, some omissions have been made for the sake of clarity. An explanation of the town and valley maps can be found on page 15 and of the piste maps on the inside back cover.

planning your trip

Once you know where you want to go, you need to decide how you want to get there. Traditionally, most skiing holidays are booked though travel agents or tour operators, but with the advent of cheap flights, DIY holidays are becoming more popular. There are pros and cons to both.

DIY v package

package

The theory behind package holidays is that all you should have to think about is getting from the top of the slopes to the bottom. The core of every package deal is convenience - though it comes wrapped in all kinds of paper. Ski companies fall into two distinct categories: large mainstream operators, and smaller more specialist ones. The mainstream brand offers ready-made holidays, where everything is already planned and you take it or leave it. Trips with smaller companies can be more expensive, but tend to be more flexible and many tailor the trip to your exact requirements. Alternatively, if you don't want to be restricted to one operator, a travel agent will have access to a selection of holidays offered by several companies.

flights - mainstream companies only run week-long trips, from Saturday to Saturday or Sunday to Sunday - giving you 6 days on the slopes and 7 nights in (or on) the town. They charter their own flights - making the holiday cheaper - but you have little option as to when or from where you travel. Smaller ski companies give you greater choice - many specialise in long weekends for the 'money-rich, time-poor' market, with departures on Thursday evenings and returns on Monday evenings, giving you 4 days skiing for 2 days off work... but the real advantage is their use of scheduled flights, so you can pick the airport, airline, and when you travel.

transfers - with a mainstream company, your journey to resort will be by coach, with others who have booked through the same company. You may have to wait for other flights, and on the way there may be stop-offs in other resorts or at other accommodation before your own. Because you're travelling at the weekend the journey tends to take longer. With a smaller company you may transfer by coach, minibus, taxi, or car depending on how much you've paid and the size of your group. And if you arrive mid-week, the transfers tend to be quicker.

accommodation - where you stay depends entirely on who you book with. Different companies have deals with different hotels, some specialise in chalets, some operate in specific resorts... the limiting factor is what's in the brochure - though if you want to stay in a particular hotel, a more specialist company may try to organise it for you.

in resort - some companies offer a drop-off and pick-up service from the lifts, which is a huge benefit in sprawling resorts. But the main benefit of a package holiday is the resort rep. From the moment you arrive to the moment you leave, there is someone whose job it is to ensure your holiday goes smoothly... or that's the theory. More than likely your rep will sort out lift passes and equipment rental. Some will organise evening activities and be available for a short period every day to answer questions. Most are supported by an in situ manager who deals with more serious issues. The more you pay for your holiday, the better your rep should be. The best are service-oriented French speakers... but it is difficult to recruit hard-working, intelligent, bilingual people to work for next to nothing. If you want to know what - or who - to expect, ask when you book.

DIY

If you DIY, you have more control over the kind of holiday you take and what you pay. But as you have to make all the arrangements, you'll need more time to plan the trip.

flights - BA, bmibaby, Swiss, and Easyjet schedule regular flights to Geneva (the best international aiport for Verbier). You can fly from all major UK airports, though the cheapest flights are normally from London, and the earlier you book the cheaper it will be. The airlines accept reservations for the upcoming winter from around June or July. Some chartered airlines such as Monarch or Thomas Cook airlines may also have a limited number of seats for sale.

If you don't want to fly, the excellent European motorway system makes driving to the Alps surprisingly easy. Getting there by train is also an option, though there may be some distance between your arrival station and your resort.

transfers - from Geneva, you can get to your resort by road and to some by train - see **travel to verbier**.

accommodation - on a DIY trip you are not restricted by brochures or company deals... however the easiest way to book a chalet or an apartment is through a company or website offering accommodation only, such as Interhome or ifyouski.com. You can liaise with the owners directly if you can find their details, but this is often difficult. For hotels you might be able to get a discount off the published price by contacting them directly.

in resort - this is perhaps where the difference between DIY and package is most noticeable. There is no rep on hand so you have to buy your own lift pass, organise your own equipment rental... but this can have its pluses: you can be sure that you get exactly the right type of pass and you can choose which rental shop you use.

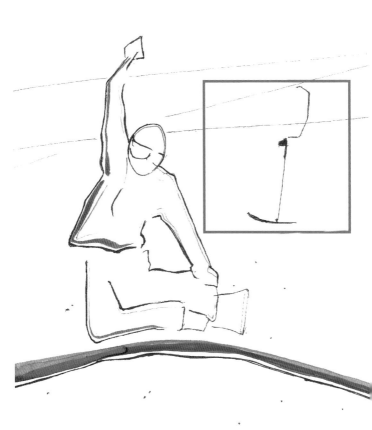

getting started

introduction

verbier val de bagnes

Verbier's rise to the top of the ski resort popularity charts has been impressive. A mere youngster compared to Wengen and Zermatt - development only boomed in the 1960s when skiing became a recreational sport for the masses - Verbier is now internationally renowned. Such is the catalogue of its charms, it is difficult to pin down a single reason for its success - whatever you look for in a skiing holiday, Verbier will provide it. Every year more and more skiers make it their destination of choice.

the resort

What is known as Verbier is actually several small villages merged together on the south-west facing plateau and lying between altitudes of 1400m and 1600m. Most of the houses are built in the chalet style so much associated with the Alps, and sprawl from as high as they dare on the avalanche-prone slopes of Savoleyres all the way across to the trees at Médran. There are few high-rise blocks to spoil the view, and despite Verbier's relative infancy as a resort, it doesn't feel purpose-built like Tignes or Flaine in France. The highest building is the distinctive Catholic church with its tall, white tower that dwarfs the other buildings and has a charm all of its own.

snapshot

highs...
- cosmopolitan atmosphere
- extensive pisted area
- excellent off-piste skiing
- expansive terrain park
- 300 days of sunshine per year on average

...and lows
- one of Europe's most expensive resorts
- limited skiing for beginners
- overcrowded slopes in peak weeks
- heavy traffic at weekends
- rarely snow on the streets

But something stops Verbier from being picture-postcard perfect - perhaps because in size the village stretches almost as far as the eye can see, or because even when the snow falls at resort level it rarely settles for long before melting. Verbier is not car-free, and at weekends the main roads through the village can become gridlocked. However, the view from the village is awe-inspiring - a 360° panorama of majestic peaks including Grand Combin (4314m) and, further afield, the Mont Blanc range. Verbier has an average of 300 days of sunshine a year, so more often than not the backdrop is a blue, cloudless sky - which is hard to beat.

introduction

who goes there

Over half the visitors to Verbier are Swiss, many coming from Geneva, Lausanne and other nearby towns for the weekend. The rest are a mix of English, German, Italian, Scandinavian and American. Verbier has a bit of a pashmina and pearls reputation and regularly attracts celebrities and royalty. While there are pockets of the cash-rich in the more up-market bars and clubs and you will spot the odd fur coat teamed with Chanel boots tottering down Rue de Médran, Verbier is not as showy as places like St. Moritz and Gstaad.

après

Verbier's après-ski and nightlife has something for almost everybody, whether your taste is for a vin chaud in the afternoon sunshine or a turn on the dancefloor in the early hours. The always busy après scene is centred on Rue de Médran, only a short walk from the end of the ski run down to the village and perfectly manageable in ski boots. If you plan to eat out, Verbier has much to offer. The wide variety of restaurants serve expensive but generally good local or international cuisine, and for those wanting something more low-key there are a few brasseries, pizzerias and cafés.

the skiing

Real skiing enthusiasts would suggest that it is the varied, demanding and apparently limitless skiing that draws people back to Verbier year after year. Verbier is the easternmost resort in the extensive 4 Vallées ski area - nearly 100 lifts link several valleys and resorts from Thyon, Veysonnaz and Nendaz, through Siviez and La Tzoumaz to Verbier. The pisted area has a huge 400km of pistes of varying degrees of difficulty, making it hard for intermediate skiers to get bored in a week's holiday. The lift system in Verbier and the 4 Vallées has a reputation for being slow, antiquated and susceptible to long queues, but in recent years TéléVerbier has improved many of the lifts around Verbier, installing newer, faster links in some of the traditional blackspots. Boarders are looked after equally well - Verbier maintains one of the biggest snowparks in the Alps.

While the attraction of the pistes may be common knowledge, not so many know that Verbier has backcountry skiing to rival the Northern American resorts and closer neighbours like Chamonix. For those in the know, and with the ability, it is Verbier's ungroomed descents that call them back. There is seemingly endless potential away from the pistes, from a brief dip into the unknown to tours lasting for days at a time.

seasonal variations

temperatures
Temperatures are easy to generalise - December and January are usually the coldest months, with things warming up through February, March and April. Don't be fooled by appearances though - it will often be colder when there is a cloudless, blue sky than when snow is falling. Temperatures can range from as low as -10°C in the resort (and colder up the mountain) on the coldest days to as high as 20°C late on in the season when the sun is shining.

snowfall

When and how much snow falls varies from year to year, but trends do emerge. In a typical year, the first snow falls on the upper slopes in October. By Christmas, there is generally enough snow cover to make all but the very lowest slopes skiable - and even these can be opened with some help from the snow cannons. The fall normally continues through January and historically the pistes have their best coverage in February, in time for the busiest weeks. As temperatures rise, levels drop again. April can be the most surprising month as there can be

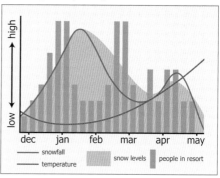

more snowfall than in March - towards the end of the season many Verbier regulars talk in eager anticipation about the 'April dump'. However, because it is normally warmer, what falls barely settles on the lower slopes before melting, and higher up the mountain it doesn't last more than a day or two.

volume of people in resort
Like other major resorts, Verbier's peak weeks are Christmas, New Year, the English and French school half terms (the middle to end of February) and Easter, when it falls early in the year. During these times, accommodation prices are at their highest and everything gets booked up months in advance. Outside of these times, special events like the Verbier Ride and O'Neill Xtreme (see **events**) make certain weekends and weeks busier than other resorts are in the same weeks. Weekends are also busy when the local Swiss flood in.

getting there

Conveniently located within easy reach of two airports and only 40 minutes from the efficient European motorway system, Verbier is one of the most accessible resorts to reach.

All contact details for the transport listed can be found in the **directory**.

by air to geneva

Another point in Verbier's favour is that the transfer from Geneva airport is noticeably shorter than to other popular resorts. Whichever form of transport you choose it should only take between 2-2½ hours.

There are daily scheduled flights to Geneva from all major UK airports - see **planning your trip**.

the airport - Geneva airport is small and easy to navigate. On your right as you come through the gate into the arrivals hall there is a small café, followed by the lost luggage counter and a small restaurant, with toilets in both directions. The short-stay car park and taxi rank are straight ahead out of the door, and Verbier is more or less straight in front of you just over 100 miles away. If you want a meal and it is daytime, there is a restaurant on the floor above departures, up the escalator.

Once you have safely landed, you can get to Verbier in one of five ways.

by hire car - you can hire a car at Geneva airport - book over the phone, on the internet, or when you arrive at the airport. Your car will have the necessary equipment such as an emergency triangle and a *vignette* (a windscreen sticker which allows you to use the Swiss motorways). You will need to specifially ask for snow chains and a roof box if you want them.

11

Verbier is approximately 105 miles (170km) from the airport along a two-lane motorway all the way to Martigny. From Geneva the journey takes just under 2 hours - though if you travel at the weekend or during the annual holidays expect traffic and delays. Leaving the airport, follow the A1 motorway towards Lausanne. At Lausanne turn onto the A9 motorway towards Montreux. Leave the motorway at Martigny taking the exit signposted to Verbier. From there follow the signs through Sembrancher to Le Châble. At the roundabout in Le Châble, take the 3rd exit up the hill to Verbier. This last part of the journey is a steep ascent up a twisty, winding road. In snowy conditions, you may need to put on chains.

by local train & bus - the train is an efficient and comfortable way to reach Verbier from the airport, and the train station is conveniently placed next to the arrivals hall. Take any train going via Martigny - on average two direct trains run every hour from early morning until just before midnight and at least one non-direct service runs every hour with a change in either Geneva or Lausanne. At Martigny change onto the Grand St. Bernard Express to Le Châble, the last stop on the line. From the station in Le Châble, the Post bus (*Car Postale*) takes you to the main bus station in Verbier on Rue de la Poste (**town b2**). The whole journey takes about 2½ hours and costs CHF55 one-way. And in a welcome change from what you may be used to, the Swiss train timetable runs seamlessly - connections between trains can seem impossibly close so you may need to find the next platform quickly.

by coach - Alpine Express, a transfer company based in Verbier, operates a shuttle service between the airport and the Place Centrale in Verbier. At the weekends, the service runs on average every 3 hours and during the week frequency depends on demand. A one-way ticket costs CHF75. Book before you arrive in Geneva.

If you are travelling in a big group, a private coach transfer may work out best - you can book one through Alpine Express, or Lemania is another reputable company.

by taxi - taxi is an expensive alternative but if you are too tired to drive there yourself or have a phobia of public transport a one-way trip

12

from Geneva airport will cost you approx. CHF650.

by helicopter - the trip from Geneva to Verbier takes about 45 minutes. One helicopter can take up to five people and costs about CHF1500. The main drawback is that it is often adversely affected by bad weather and subject to cancellation. But if arriving in style matters above all else, you can book one through Air Glaciers.

by air to sion

Sion has a small airport, which is a 40 minute drive from Verbier. Swiss operates a limited scheduled service from London Heathrow - with one flight every Saturday in each direction. From Sion you can get to Verbier by train - a service runs from Sion to Martigny twice an hour, and the journey takes about 15 minutes - or by road.

by road

The most common starting place for any road journey to the Alps is Calais. You can reach Calais from the UK by the Eurotunnel or ferry. Then by car it is just over 550 miles (just under 900 km) from Calais to Verbier - a journey that can be done in 10 hours or less. The mustard town of Dijon is about two-thirds of the way if you want to make an overnight stop along the way.

From the ferry port, take the A26 south-east to Reims, then south to

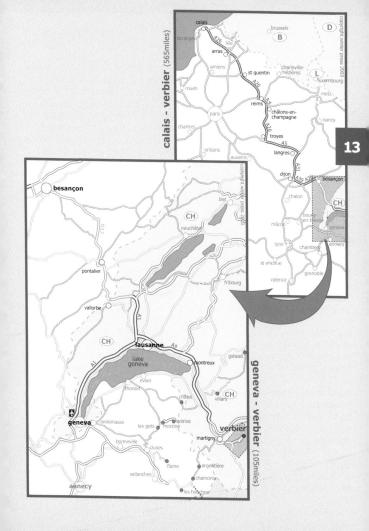

calais – verbier (565miles)

geneva – verbier (105miles)

copyright winter press 2003

copyright winter press 2003

calais
boulogne
A26
lille
arras
brussels
B
D
amiens
st quentin
charleville-mézières
L
luxembourg
rouen
A26
metz
reims
châlons-en-champagne
nancy
paris
chartres
A26
troyes
A5
orléans
langres
auxerre
dijon
A39
besançon
chalon
CH
mâcon
bourg-en-bresse
lyon
geneva
chambéry
annecy
st etienne
valence
grenoble

besançon
biel
CH
neuchâtel
pontalier
fribourg
vallorbe
A1
CH
lausanne
A9
gstaad
lake geneva
montreux
A1
evian
villars
thonon
châtel
CH
geneva
annemasse
les gets
morzine
avoriaz
verbier
bonneville
martigny
cluses
flaine
argentière
sallanches
chamonix
annecy
les houches

Troyes. From there go east on the A5 towards Langres, turning south on the A31 to Dijon. At Dijon follow the signs for the A39 and then the A36 to Besançon. At Besançon take the E23 south-west towards and into Switzerland, crossing the border just before Vallorbe. If you don't have a motorway *vignette* you can buy one here. Continuing to the end of the E23, turn south onto the A1 motorway to Lausanne. Just before Lausanne turn west along the A9 motorway towards Montreux and stay on the motorway to Martigny. From there follow the directions as under **by hire car**. There are two *péage* (toll) stops on the route south through France - you collect a ticket as you enter the motorway and then pay in cash or by credit card for your journey as you leave. Expect to pay around €50 in total for the *péage* and a *vignette*.

14

by train

In theory travelling by train gives you more time in resort - 8 days instead of the usual 6. It's an excellent service if you live in London and are skiing in the 3 Vallées or the Espace Killy, but it doesn't work out so well for a holiday in Verbier. Unless you travel by TGV, the stops in the Alps are Moutiers and Bourg St. Maurice. There isn't a direct train service to Verbier from either of these stations, so the only real way to complete your journey is by car, which is a good 3 hour drive.

If you are still undeterred, be sure to book well ahead, as the services become full months in advance.

snowtrain - the classic way to travel by train to the Alps. You check in at Dover on Friday afternoon, take a ferry to Calais where you board a *couchette* (a train with sleeping compartments) and travel overnight, arriving in the Alps on Saturday morning. The return service leaves the following Saturday evening.

eurostar overnight - this service leaves London Waterloo on Friday evenings. You travel directly to Paris, where you change onto a *couchette* to travel overnight, arriving in the Alps on Saturday morning. The return service leaves on Saturday evening.

eurostar direct - a daytime service, which leaves London Waterloo on Saturday mornings and arrives in the Alps on Saturday evenings. The return trip departs on Saturday evening.

TGV - the French intercity train system takes you closer to Verbier. A service runs from Gare de Lyon in Paris via Lausanne (where you have to change trains) to Martigny from where you can get to Verbier - see **by local train & bus**. The journey from Paris to Martigny takes around 5 hours with four services every day. To get to Paris, you can either fly or take the Eurostar.

getting around

using the maps
The guide features a number of maps to the town and valley, designed specifically for use with this guide. As with the ski maps, some omissions and changes have been made for the sake of clarity.

valley map - the valley map details the area around the town, and is contoured in the same way as the ski maps. It shows other towns, connecting roads, bus stops, train lines and highlights the area covered by the town map. It is sectioned by a grid, which is referenced throughout the guide.

town map - the inside front cover shows the town, highlighting pedestrianised zones, main buildings and landmarks, bus stops, car parks, train lines, and road names. It is sectioned by a grid, which is referenced throughout the guide.

review maps - at the end of each review section the town map is reproduced in grey, with the places reviewed shown in colour, and named on a key next to the map.

minimaps - some places reviewed are not in the town and so do not appear on the town map. Instead, they have their own small scale map (in the style of the review maps). The minimaps either enlarge a small

---

snapshot

from verbier by road
4 vallées resorts
bruson 30 mins
mayen de l'ours 1 hour 10 mins
nendaz 1 hour 20 mins
siviez 1 hour 30 mins
thyon 1 hour 30 mins
veysonnaz 1 hour 20 mins

other resorts
chamonix (france) 1 hour
courmayeur (italy) 2 hours
crans montana 1 hour 20 mins
saas fee 2 hours 10 mins
super st. bernard 50 mins
zermatt 2 hours 40 mins

15

section of the valley map or serve as an extension of the town map, and they show all relevant detail, including main buildings, bus stops and car parks.

the valley
Most skiers don't leave the village once they get to Verbier. But because of the sprawly nature of the resort you will need some transport to get between the lift stations, restaurants, shops and après. If you don't have a car you can walk, catch a bus or a taxi. If you decide when you get to Verbier that you need a car, you can hire one - see the **directory**.

on foot - the first thing you'll realise when walking around Verbier is that it has lots of hills. Shortly after that you'll realise that an efficient bus service operates in the village.

by bus - a regular, reliable and free bus service circulates Verbier from 8am to 7pm. You rarely have to wait for more than 10 minutes for a bus to turn up and in peak weeks they come more frequently though of course they are more busy. Buses loop around the resort to one of four destinations - no.1 runs to Carrefour via Savoleyres, no.2 to Le Hameau and Les Esserts, again via Savoleyres, no.3 to Patier, past the Centre Sportif, and no.4 to Verbier-Village. All buses stop at the Place Centrale and Médran. Bus stops are marked on the town and valley maps.

by taxi - an expensive way to get around Verbier, but after the free buses stop at 7pm, it can be an essential means of transport for those staying far from the village centre. The **directory** lists some of the English-speaking taxi drivers operating in Verbier or alternatively you can ask at the tourist office for a full list.

finding your way

Getting your bearings is relatively easy. The hub of Verbier is the Place Centrale where you will find the tourist office, banks, shops, restaurants, hotels and bars. The main roads in the village all begin or end at the Place Centrale.

Rue de Verbier is the way into the resort. Climbing up from Le Châble it passes through the confusingly named Verbier-Village (the original village) into modern-day Verbier and ends at the Place Centrale.

Rue de Médran is the centre of the après scene and climbs off to the right from the Place Centrale to the main lift station. Many of the hotels lie along or just off this road.

The post office and main bus station lie on Rue de la Poste, which runs west from the Place Centrale. Further along it forks to the left, and the road on the right - Rue du Centre Sportif - leads to the Centre Sportif and Patier.

To reach Savoleyres - 1 km north of the Place Centrale - take Route des Creux. Beyond Savoleyres the road splits - right for Le Hameau (and the nursery slopes) and left for the higher parts of Savoleyres and Carrefour.

driving around

If you are driving, navigating your way on these roads is relatively easy. All roads except Route des Creux are one-way, most landmarks are well signposted and traffic only builds up at weekends. Parking, on the other hand, is difficult at any time. There are large pay & display car parks at Médran and Savoleyres and the Centre Sportif (free), but very few parking spaces in the centre itself.

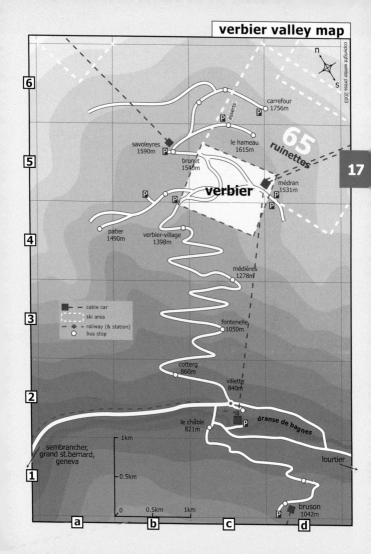

n
S

carrefour
1756m

65
ruinettes

17

esserts

P

savoleyres
1590m
P

le hameau
1615m

brunet
1540m

médran
1531m

verbier

P

P

P

pâtier
1490m

verbier-village
1398m

médières
1278m

- - - cable car
ski area
railway (& station)
○ bus stop

fontenelle
1050m

cotterg
860m

villette
840m

le châble
821m

dranse de bagnes

lourtier

sembrancher,
grand st.bernard,
geneva

1km

0.5km

0   0.5km   1km

bruson
1042m

P

a   b   c   d

accommodation

accommodation

At the end of a day on the slopes, you probably won't mind where you rest your head. But when planning your holiday, you might want to put more thought into where you stay. Verbier has the full spectrum of accommodation - 27 hotels from 2* to 5*, more catered chalets than any other resort, a few apartments and even a hostel.

18

useful information

access - little of the accommodation is ski in/ski out. If you don't have a car, and don't want to trudge around the resort in ski boots, choose somewhere near Médran or Savoleyres and/or a bus stop.

availability - accommodation is normally available from mid-December until late April, with availability best at the start and end of the season.

price - accommodation isn't cheap, but there is something aimed at all budgets. Prices rise in the peak weeks and are at their lowest at the beginning and end of the season. Staying in Le Châble or another 4 Vallée resort is a cheaper option. Package deals from the UK are only currently available to Nendaz, so for the rest you will have to arrange it yourself. Each resort has good and bad points but overall you get better value for money and access to the same ski area.

chalet, apartment or hotel

chalets
Chalet holidays cater for those who want something more relaxed, but don't want to fend for themselves.

tour operator - the most commonly available chalet package includes bed, breakfast, afternoon tea, and on 6 nights out of 7 an evening meal with wine. You will be looked after by at least one English chalet host. Mainstream operators also organise flights and transfers. The more you pay, the better you can expect the quality of everything to be. Some companies offer discounts to big groups and families. Unless you book the whole place you take pot-luck with your fellow guests - it can be a war-zone or the beginning of a beautiful friendship - but at least you know you all like snow.

The list below shows a selection of the companies offering chalet accommodation. The price brackets show an approximate figure per person for a week's holiday in mid season (including the cost of a flight).

budget (up to £500) - **skiworld**, **crystal** and **first choice** just scrape into this catagory.

mid-range (£500-£800) - **simply ski** has two chalets as does **vertical reality** who offers a b&b option.

accommodation

luxury (over £800) - **ski verbier** has the widest range, **flexiski** has two, but the cherry on the icing on the luxury cake is **descent**.

privately run - information on these chalets is not as easy to find, although the internet is a good place to start - some owners have their own websites or list their chalets on sites such as ifyouski.com. Interhome also maintains a huge database of privately-owned accommodation and lists over 30 properties in Verbier. The Verbier tourist office publishes a list for the upcoming season in mid-July of the private chalets available to rent. This gives you contact details for the chalet owner or managing agency so you can deal with them directly. Or you can contact one of the many accommodation agencies based in Verbier.

What is on offer in privately run chalets varies greatly. Some provide a similar package to those run by tour companies, some are bed & breakfast only, and in some you are left entirely to your own devices - about the only place in Verbier where you can take a room on a nightly basis is the privately run **verbier chalet**.

apartments

If an estate agent had to describe a typical ski apartment, 'compact and bijoux' would most likely be the phrase. An apartment for four is generally two rooms (a bedroom and living room), with two guests sleeping on a sofa-bed. They are on the face of it the cheapest place to stay - but when you add in the price of food and meals out, you can pay more overall than you would pay for a hotel or chalet. However if you can live like a sardine and stay disciplined about what you spend on food, it can be cost-effective.

The tourist office's list of chalets includes apartments available for short or long term let. Or again you can use one of the accommodation agencies. Some tour operators - including **ski armadillo**, **sports travel company** or **mountain beds** - rent accommodation-only apartments.

Prices vary depending upon whether it is high, mid or low season. As a guide, a short-term let for a mid-grade apartment with two rooms (four beds) costs approximately CHF2800 in peak weeks and CHF1200 in low season. Some apartments are available on a long-let if you want a place for the season. The demand is high so make sure you book early.

hotels

Each hotel has its own character and atmosphere, but they are often more impersonal than a chalet and often the more you pay, the more formal the hotel will be, from the restaurant to the service throughout. You can book directly or through a tour operator. For reviews, see **hotels**.

onto the slopes

Once you've arrived in Verbier and found where you're staying, there are a few things to do before you can get onto the slopes. For many people, long queues and language barriers make this the worst part of the holiday. The following sections take you step by step through where and when to get your lift pass, where and when to rent your equipment, and where and how to book lessons or a guide with minimum hassle.

20

lift passes

What kind of pass you buy dictates whether you find Verbier's lift pass system very efficient or very tiresome. You need your pass at the bottom of every lift in the 4 Vallées - but if you buy one for 3 days or longer it contains a microchip that is scanned automatically by the blue screen at the lift gates. You don't even have to take it out of your pocket.

verbier or 4 vallées?

Depending upon where you want to ski, you have four options. Most people buy a pass for the 4 Vallées, which covers you for all lifts within the skiable domain, from Thyon to Verbier, including Mont Fort - though beginners may only want a Verbier pass, which is good for the Lac des Vaux, Les Attelas, La Chaux, Savoleyres and Bruson areas. You can

buy a lift pass covering Savoleyres and Bruson or for Bruson only - with the latter you get one day's free use of the lifts in Champex, La Fouly, Vichères, Les Marécottes and Super St. Bernard. Any lift pass allows you to use the bus service that runs around Verbier for free.

You can buy any pass for any number of days. It is more cost effective to buy one pass valid for all the days you plan to ski, as the overall cost decreases the greater the number of days you buy it for. So if you plan to ski for 6 days it is cheaper to buy a pass for 6 days than a day pass for each day. If you decide to buy a day pass, they are cheaper after 11am (a 'midi' pass) and cheaper still if bought after 12:30pm (a 'mini' pass). If you plan to visit Verbier several times during the season, buying a season pass can be the most cost effective approach.

lift pass packages

Three little-known ski pass packages are also available. The first is the Valais Ski Card, which works on a credit basis - 1 point of credit costs CHF1, although if you buy a chunk of credit you get a discount on the price. The credit is good for 2 years and with it you can ski in 14 resorts, including the whole of the 4 Vallées, Crans Montana and Grimentz. Each day that you ski, and use a lift, credit is debited from your card.

The second package, 'Around Mont Blanc', gives you 4 days in the 4 Vallées and 2 days of your choice in either the Aosta valley in Italy (including Courmayeur and Breuil/Cervinia) and the Chamonix valley (except Les Houches) in France.

The final package is called 'Mont Blanc snow safari'. Consisting of 6 coupons you can ski in a different resort (again the 4 Vallées, the Aosta valley and the Chamonix valley) every day for 6 consecutive days.

For all these passes, you need a passport photo and to produce proof of age.

where to buy the lift passes

TéléVerbier (see the **directory**) runs and maintains Verbier's lift system and is responsible for all lift pass sales. The TéléVerbier offices at the Médran and Savoleyres lift stations open daily 8:35am-5pm. If you have booked an accommodation and lift pass package through the tourist office (see **hotels**), your pass will be waiting for you in your hotel when you arrive.

21

prices & discounts

A 4 Vallées pass is the most expensive. If you buy a Verbier pass and later decide you want to ski Mont Fort, (or anywhere else in the 4 Vallées) you can buy a supplement at the Médran and Savoleyres lift stations or on the mountain at the bottom of the Jumbo or Gentianes cable cars. Be aware that for passes of 3 days or longer, the electronic smartcard used by TéléVerbier costs CHF5 on top of the lift pass price.

Skiers between 21 and 64 years pay the full price for a lift pass. Under 21s, under 16s and over 65s qualify for discounts (of varying amounts) - and children aged 5 and under ski free (but you still need to get them a pass). You need proof of age when you buy discounted passes. For a family - of three or more including one parent - travelling together and skiing for the same number of days, a family pass is the cheapest deal. Non-skiers who want to use the lifts also get a discounted rate, as do large groups - of twenty or more - if all passes are bought at the same time for the same number of days.

You can pay with cash or credit card (Eurocard, Visa, AMEX, Mastercard and Diners).

useful information

22

photos - for ski passes for 3 days or more you need a photo - TéléVerbier can scan the picture from your passport onto the lift pass smartcard. If you come back to Verbier that year or in following seasons, you can re-use the same smartcard. If you have a Swatch watch with the Snow Pass system, your ski-pass can be loaded onto it. Lift passes are not transferable and you can be fined for using somebody else's pass - the lift operators sometimes make random checks.

queues - Saturdays and Sunday mornings are a bad time to buy your pass as the queues can be very long. You can buy a ski-pass for 3 days or more after 3pm on the day before the first day you plan to use it.

bad weather, accidents, lost & broken passes

If the lift system closes due to bad weather or any other circumstances beyond TéléVerbier's control, they will not give you a refund. Check your insurance policy as some companies provide cover for this possibility.

If you have an accident that stops you from skiing, TéléVerbier will refund the remainder of your pass. You must take it to one of their offices before 10:30am to get a refund for that day and the remaining days and you will need a copy of the medical certificate from a doctor or hospital.

If you lose a pass originally issued for 3 days or longer, or if you break your smartcard (even with a small crack the machines can't scan it), you can get a new one for a small charge.

insurance

Personal insurance against accident on the slopes is not included with your lift pass. If you have not organised your own cover before arriving in Verbier, you can buy an Air Glacier card to cover the cost of any assistance you need for on-piste incidents, including blood-wagon and helicopter recovery.

ski, boots & boards

What can often be a long-winded and tedious affair has been much improved in Verbier in recent years. Some shops are still small and stuffy, but service overall is faster and more friendly and almost all employees speak enough English to make sure you leave with what you want. As with buying your lift pass, if you avoid Saturdays and Sunday mornings, typically the busiest times, you shouldn't have to wait for hours.

equipment & price

Getting the right equipment will ensure you fully enjoy your holiday. Your feet will hurt if you don't get well-fitting boots so don't be embarrassed to persevere until you find a pair that fits. If they cause you problems on the slopes take them back - all the shops will help you find a more suitable pair. Unless you know you want a specific type or make of ski, take the advice of the ski fitter. They are the experts and will know which is the best ski for you based on your ability and age.

There is the usual extensive choice of rental shops with little difference between them. One reason to go to a particular shop is if your hotel or tour operator has arranged a rental deal with them - you may get a cheaper rate or insurance thrown in for free, so it's worth checking. Most shops stock a varied range of the latest ski equipment from all the usual manufacturers - Salomon, Völkl, Atomic, Rossignol and Dynastar. And because there are so many places to hire equipment, prices are competitive. A standard ski and boot package for 6 days costs about CHF200, whilst a premium package for 6 days costs about CHF270. Equipment for children is often available at a reduced rate - price is normally worked out on the basis of height rather than age. You can pay for your rental at the time you get your equipment or when you bring it back. If you pay upfront and then use your equipment for a shorter or longer period, the shop will make the necessary price addition or reduction when you take it back. In either case, you may have to leave a deposit and some shops may charge for ski pole hire.

insurance & security

At most shops you can take out insurance (except on test skis) to cover accidental breakage, loss or theft. Skiing on roads is not insurable! Unfortunately skis do get stolen or taken by accident - with so many people skiing on similar skis it's easy to confuse your skis with those belonging to somebody else. When you stop for lunch or après it's a good idea to swap one of your skis with a friend so you both have a mis-matched pair. This helps to ensure that nobody will pick up your skis, either by mistake or otherwise.

23

individual shops

There's little to choose between most of the shops, so the ones below are mentioned for their location, opening hours or excellent service.

skis

la boit askis (**town e3**) is close to Médran and offers free storage to its rental customers.

For skiers staying in Savoleyres, **evasion sports** (**valley b5**) on Route du Golf is the only rental shop at that end of the village.

On weekdays most shops close 12:30pm-3.00pm. **no. 1 sports** and **fellay II** (**town e4** & **f3**) both near to Médran, only close 1pm-2pm.

ski service (**town d/e3**) is part of the swissrentasport chain and lives up to its name providing excellent and fast assistance. Staff are very friendly and speak good English. You can only hire Technica boots but the range of skis is extensive.

boots

If you are looking for your own pair of boots, **surefoot** (**town e3**) makes boot-fitting an art form. They use specially-designed technology to work out the best boot for you. Once chosen they customise them to fit as you want them to.

For a more traditional approach to boot-fitting, Nick Hammond at **mountain air** (**town d/e3**) on Rue de Médran is considered by many to be the best boot fitter in Verbier.

boards

For better boards and more knowledgable service go to one of the two specialist boarding shops where the people serving you are more likely to be boarders.

hardcore (**town b2**) rents a huge range of boards, including Burton, Salomon and Rossignol, with traditional or step-in bindings, as well as a small selection of skis.

no bounds (**town d3**) rents Option, Burton, Salomon, Nitro, Buzrun, K2 or Rome boards with traditional or step-in bindings.

other equipment

Rental shops offer a lot more than just skis and boards. Most stock a wide range of ski clothing - although brands differ from shop to shop so you will need to shop around if you are looking for a specific make - and all the accessories you can think of. There is little difference from what you would pay for the same clothes in the UK.

You can also hire touring skis, telemarks, snowblades, avalanche transceivers, snowshoes... in fact more or less anything you might conceivably need or want for the great snowy outdoors.

24

ski school

ski school

Unlike the ESF in France, no single ski school holds sway in Switzerland. This has allowed the market to develop healthily - modern approaches to ski teaching compete with more traditional methods. The three schools listed cater well for English skiers and offer ski, snow-board, telemark and snowblading lessons. The general points below apply to all.

group lessons

This is the cheapest way to learn to ski. All the schools run similar systems - when you book you will be asked your level of skiing so you can be put with a group of skiers of a similar standard to yours. Skiers are split into five ability levels, which is defined by the colour of piste you are comfortable skiing on or on your own assessment of your overall standard of skiing. As a guide, level 1 is for complete beginners, level 3 for skiers who can do parallel turns on blue piste and level 5 for good skiers in all conditions. In practice the divisions are not as accurate as they could be - some people overestimate their ability or misunderstand words like 'confident´ and 'controlled', so to an extent the level of your group is pot luck. As long as you can distinguish whether you are a beginner, an intermediate, or an advanced skier you are likely to find yourself in roughly the right place. Group lessons run in the mornings and afternoons

Monday to Friday, with groups as small as three or as large as ten depending upon demand.

private lessons

If you have the money, private lessons are without question the way forward. Once you're past the basics, individual attention is the best way to significantly improve your technique and is often better value. If you can get a group of four or more the individual price is similar to the price for group lessons, with the advantage that you go where you want to go and practise what you want to practise. You can arrange where and what time you meet your instructor. If you meet at your accommodation your instructor will take you to the slopes, which at least means you'll find each other. Be aware if you ask for your 3 hour lesson to start at 10am, it will still finish at 12pm so your instructor can make his afternoon lesson.

children

You can book lessons at the schools for children aged 3 years or over - see the section on **children**.

lesson length

Private and group lessons generally last for 3 hours, 9am-12pm or 1pm-4pm. You can book a private lesson for a whole day. In low season some of the schools will book a private lesson for 2 hours.

ski school

bookings

Either book before you get to Verbier - by email, fax or phone - or once you're in resort, in person at the ski school office. In peak season always pre-book, as there are not enough instructors to meet demand. To confirm your booking, the schools will need your name, level of ability and a credit card number.

cost

Prices are fairly competitive between the schools - group lessons cost around CHF50 for a half-day and CHF200 for 5 half-days. A half-day private lesson for one or two people costs around CHF200 and CHF250 for three or four people and a full day costs around CHF350 for one or two people and CHF400 for three or four people. You can pay for your lessons in cash or by credit card. The price does not include personal insurance or a lift pass.

meeting points

All the ski schools have meeting points at Médran and Ruinettes and for beginners at Les Esserts. Make sure you check the starting point of each lesson with the ski school or instructor. Where the lesson takes place is rarely decided until the actual day, and depends on snow conditions and on the make-up of the group, so the end point will only be decided when you meet. At the end of the lesson you're on your own.

instructors

In Switzerland, ski instructors can work without any qualifications. Some schools are more stringent about hiring qualified instructors than others - to ensure you are taught by a qualified instructor ask when you book your lesson. Also due to this more relaxed policy you will find more English, Antipodean and Swedish ski instructors teaching in Verbier than in Austrian or French resorts. If you hire an instructor for a whole day, it is customary for you to buy them lunch - whether or not you tip is up to you.

refunds & cancellation

Lessons take place whatever the weather, unless the entire lift system is closed in which case the schools will refund the full lesson price. They will also refund you if you are ill or have an accident and can produce a valid medical certificate. If you cancel a lesson for any other reason, most schools will charge you 50% of the full price if you cancel at least 24 hours before the lesson. Cancel within 24 hours and the schools expect full payment.

other activities

As well as ski lessons, each school runs a programme of other activities - see **snow activities**.

« traditional »

altitude

map - town e4
t 027 771 6006
f 027 771 6111
e info@altitude-verbier.com
i altitude-verbier.com
office no.1 sports - 8:30am-1pm,
2pm-7pm, 8:30am-7pm at weekends

A new school established in 2002 by a group of Swiss and English instructors, including a former member of the UK mogul team. All of the instructors are English-speaking, coming mainly from England or Scandinavia and all of them are qualified. They train twice a week to develop their own skiing and to keep up-to-date with the latest ski techniques and teaching methods. In addition to the usual group and private lessons, Altitude runs all-female lessons with a female instructor. Or if you want to try a little bit of everything, the school offers a 'snowsport cocktail' - 3 half-days of lessons in skiing, snowboarding and snowblading. Altitude does not run telemark lessons.

la fantastique

map - town d/e3
t 027 771 4141
f 027 771 4241
e lafantastique@verbier.ch
i lafantastique.com
office rue de médran - 8:30am-12pm, 3pm-6:30pm

The supermodel of the ski schools, with instructors kitted out in distinctive red Prada ski suits and matching accessories. Private lessons are its speciality - group lessons are only available for children - and it has about 60 instructors, many of whom are English or English-speaking. It is also competent and experienced at co-ordinating lessons for corporate trips. The school's secretaries, Maryse and Veronique, are very helpful and speak reasonable English.

maison du sport

map - town b2 (main office)
t 027 775 3363
f 027 775 3369
e info@maisondusport.ch
i maisondusport.com
office médran - 8:30am-7pm
main office - 9:30am-12am, 3pm-7pm
les esserts, les ruinettes - 9am-4:30pm

The 'House of Sport' is the largest of the ski schools in Verbier - its instructors take over the resort in peak weeks. Also known as the Swiss Ski and Snowboard School, it runs all the usual lessons with particular emphasis on activities for children. Morning group lessons start at 9am, the same time as the other schools, but afternoon lessons start at 2pm. Maison du Sport is the only school to offer group lessons on Saturdays, an adult beginners lesson on Sunday mornings and lessons for handicapped skiers. The school has a large meeting point in the car park just beyond the Médran lift station. Service in the main office can be frustratingly slow, so only go when you have time to spare.

27

ski school

« an alternative »

the warren smith ski academy

t 079 359 6566 (Switzerland),
01525 374 757 (UK)
e admin@snowsportssynergy.com
i warrensmith-skiacademy.com

If you don't want to waste precious hours on lessons or spend your holiday fighting for pride of place behind your instructor the Academy offers an alternative. Warren Smith is something of a celebrity in Verbier. One of the UK's leading professional freeskiers, he is a multi-qualified instructor who established the Academy after discovering the joys of freeride. The focus is on high-performance skiing - to help intermediate or advanced skiers finesse and fine-tune their technique on moguls or steeps, in powder or when carving. The Academy runs several courses lasting for 5 days throughout the season - each day lasts 10am-3pm. Alternatively, you can book a full day or half-day private lesson. Skiers keen to qualify as instructors can use the courses as preparation and the Academy also runs race training. Peak Ski (see the **directory**), a ski company based in Verbier, offers package holidays to Verbier which include instruction with the Academy.

snapshot

lessons are for wimps

Almost every skier would benefit in some way from the odd lesson but if you would like somebody to show you around the ski area without commenting on the weaker points of your parallel turn, there are a few options.

Some UK tour operators offer a ski orientation day in their package. How often they show guests around the mountain is closely watched by the resort. The rules do change, but generally the resort allows them to guide guests on-piste once a week - the guides will not take you off-piste. It's a good way to get some inside knowledge on the best runs, the quickest lifts and the most popular watering-holes.

The Ski Club of Great Britain bases a guide in many European ski resorts throughout the season and there is one in Verbier. They run a weekly on- and off-piste ski programme for Ski Club members. Details of the different days are displayed in the tourist office and the Hotel de Verbier, where you can also meet the guide each day in the early evening.

Mountain guides will also show you around the pistes for the same price as for off-piste - just don't expect them to be too excited about it.

mountain guides

By far the best - and safest - way to make the most of the off-piste is to hire a qualified mountain guide. As they have spent years getting to know and understand the mountain terrain, not only will they find the best powder but you can trust them to look after your security.

guides v instructors
The difference is fundamental - instructing is about 'how', and guiding is about 'where'. Ski instructors are not permitted to take you off-piste and you should not ask them to. In contrast the limiting factor with a guide is your own ability.

which guide?
All qualified guides are registered with the Swiss Bureau des Guides, which effectively acts as a job agency. Most guides can also be booked through one of the ski schools. In addition there are a couple of guiding-specific companies and some independent guides - see the **directory**.

price
It's not cheap, but the bigger your group, the less you pay individually. A day's guiding for up to five people costs around CHF500. Guides can only be booked for a whole day.

useful information
equipment - unlike in France, guides are not obliged to provide you with an avalanche transceiver, but they will not take you off-piste without one. You can hire transceivers from most of the ski shops, or the ski schools may loan you one if you can charm the receptionist sufficiently.

fitness - if you decide to hire a guide, don't underestimate how fit you need to be to get the most out of the experience. Whilst the guide will cater the day to the standard of the least able skier in the group, he may still lead you along some tiring traverses or climbs to reach the best snow.

unqualified guides - perhaps because of the type of skier Verbier attracts, seasonnaires do tout their services as on- or off-piste guides. Although they may charge less than a qualified guide, you employ them at your own risk. It takes years of experience and training in mountain safety to qualify as a mountain guide and whilst unqualified guides may be excellent skiers familiar with the off-piste runs, they may not know enough about the snow conditions and the mountain environment to be able to judge whether a particular route is safe to ski or what to do if something goes wrong. There is an element of danger in all skiing, but additionally so when off-piste. For a bit more money and peace of mind, hire a qualified guide who will know how to conduct a crevasse rescue.

29

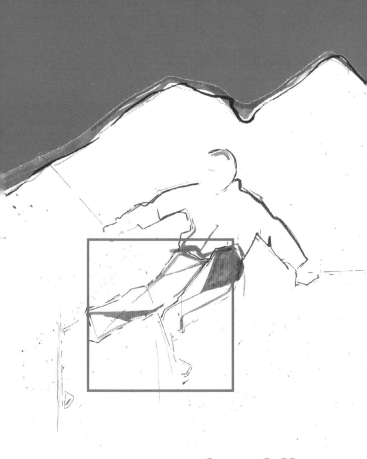

the skiing

the 4 vallées

The 4 Vallées is one of Switzerland's largest ski areas and offers everything from cruisey blues to nerve-testing high mountain tours. The size of the area, the variation of the pistes and the consistently good snow record has given the 4 Vallées a loyal following. The pistes offer most for intermediates whilst the off-piste area is a living dream for more advanced skiers and boarders.

The longest vertical drop is 2500m, but take this with a pinch of salt - it is measured from the top of Mont Fort (3300m) to Le Châble (800m). Only expert skiers will enjoy the 18km descent - it includes the black mogul field at the top of Mont Fort and a technically demanding itinerary route from Verbier to Le Châble, which is only skiable where there has been an exceptional snowfall.

pistes

A frequent complaint made about the 4 Vallées is that the the runs are badly signposted and the piste map provided by the resort is difficult to follow. The pistes are numbered on the piste map but not on the mountain, so it is not easy to work out which one you are skiing on.

You at least know when you are on a piste - the edges are marked by poles: on the left by a pole the colour of the piste with a small orange strip

snapshot

- 410 km of pistes - 30 blues, 45 reds & 10 blacks

- 95 lifts - 11 buttons, 4 cable cars, 26 chairs, 24 drags & 10 gondolas

- off-piste - 5 itinerary routes, 5 high mountain tours & vast unpisted backcountry

- highest point - 3300m

- longest run - 18km

at the top and on the right by a half orange, half piste colour pole. The lifts are named, which helps a little, and a few yellow boards show the general direction of the resorts. Otherwise little guidance is given.

The piste system adopts the same colour-coding used in all European resorts - see under 'pistes' in the **glossary** - but should only be used as a general guide. Although the gradient or width of each individual piste stays the same, other features such as snow conditions can change daily. A blue piste can become more testing than a nearby red, because it is over-crowded with skiers of ranging abilities or because of poor or icy conditions. And personal feelings about pistes vary greatly - an easy blue to one skier can seem like a vertical drop to another.

off-piste
In this guide we have distinguished between the recognised and mapped itinerary routes and high mountain tours, and the rest of the off-piste found away from the lifts that should not be ventured into without a guide.

Alongside and in between pistes in most areas you will find plenty of ungroomed snow on which to practise your technique without going too far.

lifts
The lifts in the 4 Vallées are a hotchpotch of old and new. Three companies - TéléVerbier, TéléNendaz & TéléThyon - are responsible for running and maintaining the lifts in their sector and they have different ideas about when and how much investment is required. In the last few years, TéléVerbier has made the biggest investment, so around Verbier there are more newer and faster lifts than elsewhere.

opening times - most of the lifts open in early December - the remainder being operational by Christmas - and run until the middle or end of April. The exact date changes yearly and if the snow conditions are good, the lifts may open or close earlier than advertised. The lifts open later and close earlier during the shorter daylight hours in December, January and February. In March and April they generally open half an hour earlier and close half an

hour later. Opening and closing times are noted at the bottom of each lift or you can get a full list of lift times from TéléVerbier. Wherever you ski, it is a good idea to work out which will be the last lift you will take to return home and check what time it closes.

the areas
For the purposes of this guide, the 4 Vallées has been divided into seven areas:
1 - Verbier (Attelas, Lac des Vaux & La Chaux)
2 - Mont Fort
3 - Siviez & Greppon Blanc
4 - Thyon, Mayen de L'Ours & Veysonnaz
5 - Nendaz
6 - Savoleyres & La Tzoumaz
7 - Bruson

For each, you'll find a description of how to get to and from the slopes, the general characteristics and aspect of the area, and detail of the pistes, the off-piste and the mountain restaurants (denoted by the symbol ▓). There is also a more detailed table of lift information and a piste map for each area (in which the piste colours correspond to those used by the resort). The Verbier area has two of each because of its size and the complexity of the pistes and lifts. An explanation of the lift table and the maps is on the inside of the back cover. An overview map showing how the ski areas fit together can be found on page 63.

33

where to go

beginners

The nursery slope at Les Esserts keeps first-timers - and others - amused. It is the only suitable place for complete beginners and even then some may find the button lift daunting. And because of its low altitude the piste may be entirely made of artificial snow. There is a restaurant, which serves fairly standard fare, but the 'L'-shaped terrace is an ideal spot for parents or friends to watch from.

For newcomers to skiing, the Verbier experience may seem an ordeal. Unlike more purpose-built resorts, only those staying at the higher end of the village can walk to Les Esserts. The majority will have to use the reliable bus service. However, when you are carrying skis, walking for the first time in extremely uncomfortable boots and trying to remember your goggles, gloves and hat, this can seem too much like hard work.

Beginners who have mastered the basics may find Verbier does not cater for them well either. The step from Verbier's nursery slope to Verbier's pistes is a big one - like skipping 'A' levels and going straight from GCSE to University - and whilst there are easy blue pistes in Lac des Vaux, La Chaux and Savoleyres, what you have to ski to get to them can be beyond the ability of less able or confident

beginners. And once there, getting back down to the village can be just as tricky. If you want to avoid sliding down the hill on your backside, your alternative way down is in the lift.

intermediates

By contrast the ski area is heaven for intermediate skiers. The pisted area is huge, with blue and red pistes in abundance - in a week's holiday you would be pushed to ski every one. Once you have found your ski legs, there are a decent number of black pistes on which to test your mettle.

experts

If you are an expert skier happy to hone your on-piste technique there is plenty to keep you busy. If you want to be pushed and tested at every turn, once you have skied the itinerary routes of Gentianes, Tortin and the mogul field at the top of Mont Fort, the pisted area may seem to offer little challenge. If this is the case, you would do well to hire a guide to show you Verbier's off-piste and backcountry area, which is almost as big as the pisted area.

boarders

Because it is easier to learn to board on a steep slope, novice boarders may cope better with Verbier's pistes than novice skiers and more experienced boarders will find plenty to entertain them. Skiers far outnumber boarders but because of the size of the area the two can get along quite happily. If you are a boarder who avoids drag or button lifts the Verbier sector is by far the most friendly. If you plan to explore the furthest extent of the ski area be aware that many of the essential links, especially to Thyon, are button or drag lifts, with no alternative. Getting across the area can also be tiresome as there are several long, flat paths. The same is true of the links to and from Nendaz - you must use two drag lifts.

the snowpark

The main attraction for boarders - and some skiers - is the SWATCH-sponsored boarderX (pronounced cross) at La Chaux. Allegedly there is also a snowpark under the Tournelle chairlift in the Savoleyres area and a half-pipe at Col des Gentianes, but these are not always maintained or usable - check with TéléVerbier for info on their status or existence.

non-skiers

As a non-skier, the first good reason to go up the mountain is to admire the spectacular view in every direction, while the second is to walk along the groomed and marked footpaths (of which there are over 25km in total). With a lift pass - see **getting started** - you can go up in any of the gondolas or cable cars, but not the chairlifts, drags or button lifts for obvious reasons. Wherever you walk, watch for out-of-control skiers - or tobogganers - flying past.

The starting point is Médran, the same as for skiers - take either gondola to Ruinettes. Once there you have three choices. You can go higher in the Attelas gondola and follow the path from there to the top of the Chassoure-Tortin gondola in which you can descend to Tortin. Another option is to walk down from Ruinettes along the blue piste which runs through the forest to Médran. The third walking route is from Ruinettes to La Chaux or you can take the strange caterpillar-tracked bus that runs between the two points - it is for pedestrians only and runs 9am-4pm. Once in La Chaux, it would be a shame not to carry on to the top of Mont Fort - take the Jumbo and then the Mont Fort cable car - to the large viewing platform from where you can admire the stunning vista of peaks. Once a week TéléVerbier organises a trip to the top for sunrise.

On the Savoleyres side, once up the mountain in the Savoleyres gondola you can descend to La Tzoumaz in its gondola or walk down to the Sky Bar. From Carrefour, you can walk up the route of the same name - if it is open - to Marmotte. If your legs need a break by the time you get back down the no.1 bus runs from Carrefour to the centre of Verbier.

the ski areas

where to start

The Médran lift station is the starting point in Verbier for all the skiing in the 4 Vallées except for the Savoleyres and Bruson areas. All the village buses stop in front of Médran.

If you come by car there are two car parks just beyond the lift station on either side of the road, which are pay & display between 8am and 4pm. At weekends the road to Médran becomes clogged with traffic, as visitors from Lausanne, Geneva and elsewhere pour into Verbier, meaning there is rarely a space in the car parks after 10am - so get there early.

the first lift

From Médran, you can get up the mountain in either of the inspirationally named gondolas, Médran 1 or Médran 2 - the latter starts in Le Châble. Both finish at 2200m at the mid-station known as Ruinettes. The entrance for the gondolas is the same - at the far end of the lift station if you approach it from the village - and opens at 8:45am. From that time until 11am at weekends and in peak weeks you can wait for up to 40 minutes to get into a lift. One way to bypass the queues is to do the round-trip down and back from Le Châble in the Médran 2 gondola - this is often quicker than standing in the queue - and always more pleasant, as you are guaranteed a seat.

les attelas, lac des vaux & la chaux

Above the eastern end of the village lie the three distinct valleys of Lac des Vaux, Attelas and La Chaux, known collectively as 'Verbier'. They are all shown on the same map (page 67) with the exception of the lower slopes in Attelas, below the Ruinettes mid-station. These slopes appear on the map on page 65 and are used most commonly at the end of the day as a return to Médran.

les attelas map p.65 & 67

The main valley is known as Attelas - its pistes start as high as 2723m and run all the way down past the Ruinettes mid-station to Verbier. It is by far the busiest valley of the three - in the morning all skiers use its lifts to reach Lac des Vaux, La Chaux, Nendaz, Siviez and Thyon and then ski its pistes at the end of the day to return from these areas to the town. When Route Carrefour is open skiers returning from Savoleyres also ski the lower pistes below Ruinettes. The upper pistes are graded red or black, so only reasonably competent (or confident) intermediate skiers will cope with them and at the end of the day they can be littered with struggling skiers.

aspect

Most of the slopes in Attelas face south-west. Combined with the volume of traffic, conditions in this area are generally poorer than elsewhere, particularly below Ruinettes. There are several snow-making machines, which work hard to keep snow levels topped up - but even with these the pistes can be poorly covered at the end of day or the beginning or end of the season.

getting there

From Médran, take either gondola to Ruinettes. From there to reach the top take the Funispace or Attelas 2 gondola, the latter being slower but often quieter. Both end on the ridge between Lac des Vaux and Attelas, though at slightly different points.

the pistes

blue - the only one in the area is the gentle path that runs through the forest from Ruinettes down to Médran - see **getting down**.

red - Attelas has red pistes galore. The main descent from the top of Attelas is red - you can reach it from the top of the Funispace or the top of the Attelas 2 gondola - and offers a range of routes down. Coming from the top of the Funispace, the left side is a narrow flatish path whilst the right side is a steep wide slope. Lower down it splits - the left route is steep and often icy whilst the right is a narrow path. From there the piste continues all the way down to the bottom of the Combe 2 chairlift, although along the way you can turn

---

snapshot

- highest point - 3023m

- aspect - sw

- lifts - 4 buttons, 7 chairs & 4 gondolas

- pistes - 1 blue, 3 red & 2 black

- off-piste - 1 itinerary route & 2 high mountain tours

- restaurants - 6

37

---

off to La Chaux or to Ruinettes. Being the only way to ski down to Verbier, the generally heavy traffic and consistently poor snow conditions on the lower section doesn't make this a piste you ski for enjoyment's sake. However, if you do want to ski the upper part again it is better to go back up in the Combe 2 or Attelas 3 chairlifts as both are normally quieter than the lifts from Ruinettes. The piste from the top of Combe 2 is also red, a flat and narrow path to start with before widening into a fairly steep slope.

The lower reds to the bottom of the Mayentzet and Combe 1 chairlifts are ideal for intermediates wanting to do laps to practise their technique.

black - there are two in this area. The first and longest is narrow and steep - it starts at the top of the

Funispace, sweeping down Attelas from underneath this lift to the bottom of the Mayentzet chairlift. The first 20 metres or so can be bare or heavily mogulled, but beyond that the run is smooth and fast. The piste is often used for competitions during which time it is closed to the public.

38

The second black is shorter and starts just below Ruinettes, although the top section is not always groomed. It also ends at the bottom of the Mayentzet chairlift.

off-piste
itinerary routes - the only one starts at the top of the Fontenay chair. A relatively short descent it is often mogulled but is a good place to test your technique without exhausting yourself before trying the longer, more testing Gentianes and Tortin routes.

high mountain tours - for expert skiers, the majestic Mont Gelé peak that dominates Attelas is the main draw. To reach the top, take the Mont Gelé cable car, which starts next to the top of the Funispace. The lift closes in high winds or when the conditions on this notoriously testing mountain are too difficult or unsafe. From the top you can ski the most popular route - down towards Tortin - or the south face to La Chaux. The extreme couloirs visible from Attelas are rarely skied, except during the Verbier Ride (see **events**), when professional freeriders hurtle down at unbelievable speeds.

other - as you ascend in the Funispace, you will notice several extreme couloirs. Known as Creblet and Rock and Roll these descents are for true experts and though you'll see the tracks, you'll rarely see the skier.

lunch
attelas
1 **t** 027 771 3291
A small self-service restaurant at the top of the Attelas 2 gondola. The outside terrace is perfect for soaking up the sun under the gaze of Mont Gelé. During the Verbier Ride (see **events**), it is used by the event organisers and members of the press.

au mayen
7 **t** 027 771 1894
A small, rarely busy restaurant the name of which means 'home'. Sadly the service doesn't live up to the name, often being unfriendly and slow, even when there are only a handful of diners, but it is worth going for the excellent *croûte* - a local dish of bread, cheese and ham.

carrefour (see page 84)
8 **t** 027 771 7010
The restaurant lies at the end of bus route 1, but you can ski there from Attelas and from Savoleyres if Route Carrefour is open.

chez dany
9 **t** 027 771 2524
A Verbier institution - known to many, but because of its location elusive to

some. Nowhere else can you sample the friendship 'coffee' (*grolla*), which from its unashamedly alcoholic taste seems unlikely to have passed close to a coffee bean. It is a very popular lunch-stop, so book a table - there are hourly sittings from 12:30pm to 3:30pm. To ski there, take the narrow, winding red piste from the bottom of the Ruinettes chair, turning left at the signpost to Chez Dany. Follow the itinerary route (and the hundred or so ski tracks before you) through the forest to the small hamlet of Clambin. Beginners or timid intermediates may find the route beyond their ability and the restaurant is only accessible when the snow is plentiful. A ski-doo is the best option to get there in the evening, and you can sledge home to Médran. Call to check they are open before you head up the mountain, as if there are no bookings they won't open. And take lots of cash, as no credit cards are accepted.

2 l'olympique
t 027 771 2615

The building adjacent to the top of the Funispace houses two restaurants under the same name. Downstairs is self-service with large seating areas inside and outside on the south-facing terrace. The food is varied and good, but expensive. Upstairs has waiter service inside and out - the menu offers a selection of tasty salads, pasta, risotto and polenta preceded by a delicious appetiser of brown

bread and tapenade. Reservations are essential. When it is sunny, fondue and crêpes are available upstairs on another small terrace.

5 & 6 ruinettes
t 027 771 1979

The waiter-service restaurant upstairs receives good reviews, whilst the self-service restaurant downstairs is very mediocre and over-priced. A better option for a cheap quick lunch is the kiosk lower down the slope, which sells a selection of sandwiches.

getting home

on skis - the only way to ski to the village is along the quite narrow but gentle blue path from the bottom of the Mayentzet chair, which winds through the forest. At the end of the day it is like the M25 in the rush-hour, not only with skiers and toboganists flying past at various speeds, but also pedestrians and dogs. Conditions can be poor and in late season or little snow it is often closed. The path starts at Ruinettes, or you can join it lower down by first skiing a red - fast and wide - or a black - fast and often icy - piste, both of which join the blue at the bottom of the Mayentzet chair.

by lift - when the path is closed because of poor snow below Ruinettes, you can descend to the village in the Médran gondolas.

39

lac des vaux map p.67

Lac des Vaux is a minature ski resort in itself, which - thanks to being a sheltered bowl - often seems to escape the worst of the weather. The vertical drop is quite short, but the area offers one piste of each colour and the start of two high mountain tours. All pistes end at the bottom of the two lifts, Lac des Vaux 1 and Lac des Vaux 3, so mixed ability groups can happily ski here together, safe in the knowledge that nobody will get too lost.

40

aspect
As the slopes face north-west, conditions stay generally good throughout the season.

getting there
From the village take either Médran 1 or 2 to Ruinettes and from there either the Funispace or Attelas 2 gondola. Lac des Vaux lies on the left side of the ridge at the top of either of these lifts.

pistes
blue - Lac des Vaux's one blue piste is a gentle and wide descent reachable from the top of the Funispace and Attelas 2 gondola. The approach from the Funispace is narrow and busy, so take some care. You can also reach the piste from the top of the Attelas 2 gondola - follow the signs to Lac des Vaux along a narrow path which forks to the left.

snapshot

- highest point - 2740m

- aspect - nw

- lifts - 2 chairs

- pistes - 1 blue, 1 red & 1 black

- off-piste - 1 itinerary route & 2 high mountain tours

- restaurants - 1

red - the one red piste is reached by turning right at the top of Lac des Vaux 3 - left takes you to the top of the Tortin itinerary route. Initially it is quite narrow and steep but widens out after about 50 metres. Lower down it crosses the blue run, ending at the start of Lac des Vaux 1 and 3.

black - graded black but really just a tricky red, this piste is reached by turning right at the top of Lac des Vaux 1 - ski beneath the Funispace building - or from the top of the Funispace. It splits halfway down - the descent on the right is smooth and fast whilst the descent on the left is shorter but more challenging and often mogulled. A short run, it joins the red piste lower down.

off-piste
itinerary routes - from the top of Lac des Vaux 3, you can reach Tortin, Verbier's most infamous route (also

see the Mont Fort map on page 69). Spoken of in hallowed terms, this is often the target (and the nemesis) of many a skier's visit to Verbier. From the top you are treated to a vista of a long, steep drop, often with moguls the size of VW Beetles. For many the worst part is making the first turn - but once you're moving the descent is exhilarating. Conditions on Tortin are variable and change every day. As the season progresses or snowfall is infrequent, more and bigger moguls develop. The bottom half is a path, which can be bare in late season or when there has been little snow. To return to Lac des Vaux, take the Chassoure-Tortin gondola.

high mountain tours - Lac des Vaux is the gateway to two high mountain tours, Vallon D'Arbi and Col de Mines. The main entry to the top of both of these routes is through a gap in the wire fence just above Lac des Vaux 1 (as you ski down the mountain). The upper part of both tours follows the same route, along a path hugging the contours of the mountain with a steep drop-off on the right. Boarders won't enjoy the long and undulating traverse. The routes then split, as indicated by a yellow board. Vallon d'Arbi is very scenic, it runs down the right side of the mountain through the trees to finish in La Tzoumaz - if you're lucky you may see some chamois. Col de Mines is particularly avalanche-prone with spectacular views over Verbier. It runs

down the left (and south facing) side of the mountain coming out at the bottom of Attelas. The entrance to the routes will be closed if TéléVerbier thinks they are unsafe to ski. As elsewhere, respect the signs.

lunch

2 **l'olympique** (see page 39)
t 027 771 2615
L'Olympique is reached by turning right at the top of Lac des Vaux 1.

getting home

on skis - once you are in Lac des Vaux, the only way to return to the top of the ridge between it and Attelas is to take Lac des Vaux 1. From the top you can ski into Attelas and from there, all the way down to the village.

Most people who have spent the day skiing in the 4 Vallées return to Verbier up the Chassoure-Tortin gondola through Lac des Vaux. If it is late and you notice Lac des Vaux 1 is closed as you ski towards it, take the left fork half-way down the red piste along a narrow path (uphill at the end), which takes you to the top of Attelas.

by lift - once you have got to the top of Lac des Vaux 1, beginners or timid Intermediates can get back down to the village by taking the Funispace or Attelas gondola and then either Médran gondola.

la chaux map p.67

La Chaux, similar to Lac des Vaux, is a self-contained area of blue and red pistes making it ideal for beginners, cautious intermediates and children. It is also popular with the ski schools. Towards the end of the season its hills are a good place for a bit of marmotte spotting.

aspect

As La Chaux has a lower altitude than Lac des Vaux, and as the pistes face south the snow conditions are less consistently good. The top section can be icy in the morning, whilst later on in the season or in the afternoons of warmer days, slushy conditions or bare patches develop more quickly here than elsewhere.

getting there

You can reach La Chaux from various points on Attelas. From the top of the Funispace or the Attelas 2 gondola, ski down the red piste into Attelas to the first fork on the left (about 1/3 of the way down before you reach the bottom of the Attelas 3 chairlift) - this takes you down a narrow path to the top of one of the red pistes into La Chaux. If you are lower down on Attelas, the La Combe 2 chairlift takes you to the top of the ridge between Attelas and La Chaux and the top of the other red run into La Chaux. If you are only as high as Ruinettes you can get to La Chaux on the Fontenay chairlift - reached by skiing along the

snapshot

• highest point - 2485m

• aspect - s

• lifts - 2 chairs

• pistes - 2 blue, 2 red & 0 black

• off-piste - none

• restaurants - 1

blue path from Ruinettes. The chair finishes on the ridge between Attelas and La Chaux and the start of one of the blue pistes down into La Chaux.

pistes

blue - there are two blue pistes. One runs from the top of La Chaux 2 and the other runs from the top of the Fontenay and La Chaux 2 chairlifts along one edge of the Snowpark. Both end at the bottom of La Chaux, and are gentle and wide.

red - the reds into La Chaux are living proof of why the piste colour coding system should only be used as a guide. There are only two, one reached from the top of La Combe 2 and the other by turning left at the top of La Chaux 2 or at the end of the La Chaux approach path from Attelas. Whilst the lower section of both will pose few problems, negotiating the top of each is more tricky. Both are steep, and sometimes mogulled, with either icy or slushy conditions and rarely anything in between these extremes.

the snowpark

For snowboarders keen to practise some tricks, the attraction of La Chaux is the excellent and well maintained Snowpark, with a variety of jumps, rollers and rails. As you look up the valley you will see a large area on the left side specially reserved for the park. The entrance is under the top of the La Chaux 1 lift, from where a short traverse to the left leads to the initial kickers.

Everything in the park has a flag next to it to indicate its difficulty, though you can probably tell just by looking that the little stuff is for beginners, the medium sized stuff is for intermediates, and the big stuff is for experts. The three lines through the park - one for each level - lead to an assortment of hits and the odd rail to grind… and the freestyle slope has a variety of different sized jumps. The snack shack at the bottom sells drinks and BBQ'd food to the accompaniment of a pumping sound system.

off-piste

No off-piste routes start from La Chaux, but quite a large part of the terrain in between the pistes is left ungroomed, and is somewhere to get a taste of gentle off-piste skiing after a dump of powder.

lunch

3 **la chaux**
t 027 778 1535

Most of the seating is outside - the inside area is small and spartan - so only stop here for lunch on a sunny day. Both quality and choice are pretty standard. For hot food order at the left hatch - you're given a number and they announce when your meal is ready over the tannoy - or if you only want drinks, chocolate and cold snacks, queue up at the right-hand hatch.

43

getting home

on skis - both the chairlifts in La Chaux take you to a point where you can ski into Attelas and then back down to the village.

by lift - you can't get back to the village by lift only - whichever lift you take out of La Chaux, you have to ski at least as far as Ruinettes from the top of it. Once there you can descend to the village in either of the Médran gondolas.

mont fort map p.69

At 3330m, Mont Fort is the highest skiable peak in the 4 Vallées. The panorama at the top is quite literally breathtaking - and not just because of the altitude. On a clear, sunny day you can see Mont Blanc and the Matterhorn, as well as the lesser-known peaks of Rosablanche and Grand Combin. The more immediate view is of a seemingly endless off-piste area where expert skiers descend what look like vertical drops. As it demands superb technique, and shouldn't be attempted without a guide, most people head for Mont Fort's steep black mogul run instead. Ranking a close second to Tortin in terms of infamy, the debate rages as to which is steeper or harder.

aspect

The whole area is on a glacier so unless you are with a guide - who knows where the crevasses are - stay on the pistes. Because of the glacier and the high altitude, it can be colder up here than in other areas.

getting there

The most direct route from Verbier is through La Chaux up the Jumbo. If you are at the Tortin mid-station, take the Gentaines cable car. To ski Mont Fort you need a 4 Vallées pass - if you don't have one you can buy a Mont Fort extension at the bottom of the Jumbo or Gentianes cable cars.

snapshot

- highest point - 3330m
- aspect - sw, w & nw
- lifts - 3 cable cars, 3 drags & 1 gondola
- pistes - 0 blue, 4 red & 1 black
- off-piste - 1 itinerary route
- restaurants - 4

the pistes

red - Mont Fort's red pistes are of varying degrees of excitement. The run from the top of the Jumbo down to La Chaux is long, winding and fairly dull - it is a path in all but one short section. Most people only ski it to get back to La Chaux or to Cabane du Mont Fort for lunch. The wide, red pistes from the Glacier draglifts and the top of the Jumbo are more fun and ideal for carving practice.

black - the steepest black in the 4 Vallées starts at the top of the Mont Fort cable car. Once down the steps, you face a sea of moguls. Those at the top tend to be the worst, as skiers fall into the 'follow-the-tracks' trap to get over them, which causes unskiable bumps to form. The lower half is more regularly groomed, making it smoother and faster with one lip from which - if you want - you can get some air.

off-piste

itinerary routes - the Gentianes route starts just below the Glacier draglifts. Whichever way you get down it will be long and testing and probably mogulled. Less popular than Tortin, the conditions are generally better and the traffic lighter. The lower section is a path which can be bare in spots. Gentianes ends at the Tortin mid-station where you can take the Chassoure-Tortin gondola to the top of Tortin or return to Mont Fort by the Gentianes cable car. For details of Tortin see **lac des vaux**.

other - Mont Fort is where the true off-piste kicks off - Stairway to Heaven, Highway, Catwalk, Jacob's Ladder and Backside are all reached from here. However, don't go looking for them without a guide. Mont Fort is flanked by the Bec des Rosses, but you'll probably only see skiers on its steep and rocky sides during the O'Neill Xtreme (see **events**).

lunch

4 cabane du mont fort
t 027 771 7191
A very popular lunch-stop perched on an outcrop off the piste down to La Chaux. Inside can feel over-cosy when busy, and the food can take time to arrive. On sunny days, crowds flock to the south-facing terrace causing long queues. Historically a refuge - have a look at the doors in the back wall - you can still stay overnight but you must book (027 778 1384).

2 cabane du tortin
t 027 288 1153
Jutting out on a rock under the shadow of Mont Fort, this small restaurant is a short walk from the top of the Glacier draglifts - turn left at the top. Because of its location, it is often undeservedly quieter than worse places - the food served is wholesome and well-priced.

3 col des gentianes
t 027 778 1505
No prizes for food or for service here. The best thing is the large terrace, which is ideally placed for enjoying the sun or for watching the O'Neill Xtreme (see **events**).

1 la chotte de tortin
t 027 288 1153
A reasonable self-service restaurant at Tortin. Inside is small and over-warm, and queues can be very long because of the cramped counter system. The seating area outside is large, and is a real sun-trap for a few hours in the middle of the day. Credit cards are accepted for a minimum of CHF20.

getting home

on skis - the quickest way down is on the red piste to La Chaux, from where you can take either chair back to Attelas.

by lift - the Jumbo takes you as far as La Chaux and then either chair takes you to the top of Attelas. Once there you have to ski to Ruinettes.

siviez & greppon blanc
map p.71

Also known as 'Super-Nendaz', Siviez is a small, fairly ugly hamlet. Most skiers from Verbier pass through only fleetingly on their way to the rest of the skiing in the 4 Vallées. Greppon Blanc is the name given to the slopes on the east side of Siviez. Also used mainly as a thoroughfare by skiers to get between Thyon and the rest of the 4 Vallées, the pistes are consequently quieter than those in other areas, and in low season you can have some slopes all to yourself.

aspect
The pistes in Greppon Blanc face west and always seem to be blessed with sunshine. Despite this, the snow conditions here are often better than in other areas, perhaps helped by the generally high altitude - most pistes lie above 2200m - and the overall lower volume of skiers.

getting there
The quickest way from Verbier is through Lac des Vaux, up Lac des Vaux 3 and down Tortin. Once there, take the Tortin chairlift across the flat plateau, coming off at the hut at the top of the blue piste down to Siviez. To use this lift and those that follow you need a 4 Vallées lift pass. The Noveli chairlift, which starts on the other side of the car-park in Siviez, is the link to the Greppon Blanc pistes.

snapshot

- highest point - 2643m
- aspect - w
- lifts - 3 chairs & 5 drags
- pistes - 1 blue, 7 red & 2 black
- off-piste - 1 high mountain tour
- restaurants - 3

the pistes
blue - the only blue is the run from Tortin to Siviez. Lower down, it can be slushy or bare from over-use.

red - Greppon Blanc takes the crown with the most varied and exciting red runs of any area. The longest piste runs from the top of Noveli down to Siviez and is wide and quite speedy. The red from the top of Greppon Blanc 1 starts off as a flat path - annoyingly for boarders, who will end up walking - before sweeping down the mountain. It splits just before the bottom of the Greppon Blanc 3 chair - left to the bottom of the Meina drag or back towards Siviez and right towards Piste de L'Ours and Thyon or the Chottes drag. Intermediates will enjoy these pistes, being wide and long enough to get up some decent speed for some carving turns.

black - there are two blacks, but if you have just skied Mont Fort's moguls you may question their rating, as neither is as long nor as testing. One black runs alongside the Greppon Blanc 2 drag - turn right at the top to reach it - and must be so rated only because it can be icy in the morning. The other starts at the top of Greppon Blanc 3 and is steeper, but shorter.

off-piste
high mountain tours - the Eteygeon high mountain tour starts a short hike from the top of the Greppon Blanc 3 chair or the Greppon Blanc 1 drag. Amazingly the route ends in the middle of nowhere, but from time to time a man in a van turns up to take you to the Les Masses chair near Thyon.

lunch
aux chottes
2 **t** 079 652 4542
A large, attractive restaurant halfway down the draglift of the same name. Inside there is waiter service and the best table is under the eaves up a small ladder. Outside there are two terraces - the smaller one has the same menu and waiters as inside, whilst the larger one is standard self-service.

chez odette
3 **t** 027 288 1982
Chez Odette is the main reason to spend any time in Siviez. An extremely friendly place serving excellent food, you are welcomed with an apéritif - ingredients unknown

- and fed from a delicious menu of local specialities.

combatzeline
1 **t** 027 288 2041
A reasonable self-service restaurant next to the top of the chairlift. Its biggest attraction is the sun-baked south-facing terrace.

For arguably the best vin chaud in the 4 Vallées, stop at the market stall in Siviez.

getting home
on skis - it's not a short ski so reserve some energy. Taking the top of the Chottes drag as the starting point, the way home is along the red piste on the left side of the Meina draglift. Halfway down take the left fork along a track signposted Siviez, which leads to the Greppon Blanc 1 & 2 drags. Take no.2 - you can come off half-way if you're short of time - and ski the red piste down to Siviez. Once there the quickest way home is up the Tortin chairlift, Chassoure-Tortin gondola, through Lac des Vaux and down through Attelas.

by lift - the weary won't want to know that you can't return to Verbier by lift alone. To get down to Siviez, you have to ski, as above in **on skis**. Once in Siviez, the rest of the journey is by lift - Tortin, Chassoure-Tortin, Lac des Vaux 1, the Funispace and a Médran gondola - except for a little skiing through Lac des Vaux.

thyon, mayen de l'ours & veysonnaz map p.73

Thyon is the furthest resort from Verbier. A modern and characterless place, which has a more Germanic feel although it is still just in French-speaking Switzerland. Entirely purpose-built, even the layout of the lifts feels entirely functional, and you'll rarely find a bump on any of the pistes.

48

Veysonnaz and the prettily-named Mayen de L'Ours ('home of the bear') lie at the north end of the Thyon valley. The villages are more attractive and the pistes more exciting than those in the rest of the valley.

aspect

The runs around Thyon mainly lie between 1800m and 2450m, and because of their generally high aspect, the conditions stay good. There are plenty of snow cannons to keep levels topped up. The villages of Mayen de L'Ours and Veysonnaz lie at 1400m, so despite the snow cannons, conditions can be poor to the bottom of the runs.

getting there

The way from Verbier is up through Lac des Vaux, down Tortin to Siviez and up into Greppon Blanc. Once you get as far as the piste down to the Chottes draglift, follow the signs to the Piste de L'Ours, along the path that forks off to the right of the red

piste. You need a 4 Vallées lift pass to ski here.

the pistes

blue - too many to mention individually, Thyon's blues criss-cross in a spider's web pattern. None of them are particularly exciting, and most are wide and fairly flat. The main purpose of their layout seems to be convenience rather than fun.

red - the long, twisting red runs down to Mayen de L'Ours and Veysonnaz are the main attraction in this area. Both start at the same point just above Thyon and wind their way down through the forest, with sweeping turns and enjoyable rollers. The bottom of the runs are low and can be poorly covered when the snow conditions are poor or the weather is warm. If skied without stopping you will feel like you've had a real workout by the time you reach the bottom. Two other, reasonably fun red pistes run alongside the two drags - Cheminée and Les Cretes - whilst another leads to the Tsa drag. A little steeper than the blue pistes in the area, they are also more narrow.

black - the area's one black piste runs underneath the Etherolla chairlift and will make you wonder whether Thyon applies a different piste grading system - it's a longish but unchallenging descent.

off-piste

There are no itinerary routes or high mountain tours in the area, but the piste bashers don't groom all the snow in between the runs if you are looking for some gentle 'off-piste'.

lunch

There are a number of restaurants on the pistes and in the resorts themselves. However, unless you are staying near Thyon or are travelling back to Verbier by road, eating lunch around Thyon may leave you short of time to ski back to Verbier. A better idea is to eat lunch at one of the restaurants in the Greppon Blanc area on your way home.

1 **mont rouge**
t 027 281 3195
Probably the only place you should stop for lunch and only because of its location at the bottom of the Cheminée draglift - this takes you to the top of the run back to Greppon

Blanc. A long barn-like restaurant, it has a self-service counter serving average food and a small room with waiter service, and slightly better and more expensive cuisine.

other

At the bottom of Piste de L'Ours, you will find an igloo-shaped glass building, creatively named the **igloo**. A welcome sight if you skied the piste without stopping, it is an ideal refreshment spot where you can sit ouside and admire what you've just come down.

There are 2 restaurants - **remointze** and **les caboulis -** on the long red piste down to Veysonnaz. Both have terraces and waiter service.

getting home

on skis - wherever you have been skiing in the area, the route home is the same - take the Cheminée draglift out of Thyon and at the top ski down the red run to the Tsa draglift, which brings you into Greppon Blanc, to the top of the piste leading to the bottom of the Chottes draglift. At the top of this lift, the route home on skis is the same as for **siviez & greppon blanc**.

by lift - as for **on skis**, once you have got to the top of the Chottes draglift, the route home by lift is the same as for **siviez & greppon blanc**.

49

nendaz map p.75

Nendaz is promoted as an ideal destination for newcomers to skiing, and certainly the runs at the top of the Tracouet gondola are a paradise for beginners and families. However, unless you are staying in Nendaz, skiers with less ability will find the ski there from Verbier far less pleasurable or even do-able. On skis, the only way to get to Nendaz from Verbier is down Plan du Fou, where the descent is a short itinerary route followed by a grotty black run. Although you can descend in the Plan du Fou gondola to miss out the itinerary, skiing the black is unavoidable.

And that is not where Nendaz's problems stop. Another less attractive aspect is the lifts. Some of them have been in place for many years and so feel somewhat antiquated. The conditions are consistently the worst in the 4 Vallées and the snow-making facilities on this side of the mountain are limited so those slopes most exposed to the sun often suffer from poor coverage.

aspect
The pistes in Nendaz face in a range of directions from east, through north to west and so have a range of conditions.

getting there
The route to Nendaz from Verbier is

snapshot

• highest point - 2430m

• aspect - e, ne, n & w

• lifts - 2 buttons, 1 cable car, 2 chairs, 5 drags & 1 gondola

• pistes - 6 blue, 2 red & 1 black

• off-piste - 1 itinerary route

• restaurants - 2

the same as for the route to Siviez - up Attelas, through Lac des Vaux, down to Tortin and then Siviez. The link from Siviez is the Siviez chair, which starts just behind the bottom of the Tortin chairlift. You need a 4 Vallées lift pass to use the lifts in this area.

the pistes
blue - the pistes around the top of Tracouet are all short and easy blues, with lots of space in which to practise and re-practise snowplough turns. For a longer run, you can ski all the way down to Nendaz on a flatish blue piste that passes through the forest. On the way home back to Verbier the piste from the top of the Siviez chair is also a blue and a track in parts.

red - there are only two in the whole area. One, a reasonably short, unexceptional run, starts from the top of Plan du Fou down the Siviez side to the bottom of the Plan du Fou draglift. The red on the Nendaz side is signifcantly longer - it starts at the top of the Dent button lift and winds all the way down to the town. Conditions towards the bottom can be poor.

black - the area's one black run, from the bottom of the Plan du Fou cable car, feels Nendaz's lack of snow-making facilities the most. The conditions here are generally poor, which probably explains its rating. It is not as technically difficult as other blacks in the 4 Vallées, but you need to be confident that your ability will help you avoid the bare spots and rocks that litter the surface throughout the season.

off-piste
itinerary routes - the only one in the area is a short, but steep descent from the top of the Plan du Fou cable car. If you've comfortably skied Tortin or Gentianes it will seem like a walk in the park.

lunch
1 plan du fou
t 027 288 3367
A circular, glass-panelled restaurant at the top of Plan du Fou. On a clear day the 360° panorama is stunning. The goulash soup receives plaudits but unless you get there within typical lunch hours you may find little food left or that service has stopped altogether.

2 tracouet
t 027 288 2341
Every side of the mountain has one and this is Nendaz's - it looks like a functional, atmosphereless self-service restaurant and does not try to beat expectations. But unless you want to ski down to Nendaz it's the only real choice.

getting home
on skis - the initial stretch of the descent from the top of Plan du Fou to Siviez is red and then becomes blue. Once in Siviez, there's no more skiing until you reach the top of the Chassoure-Tortin gondola into Lac des Vaux. From there you can ski through Lac des Vaux and Attelas to Verbier.

by lift - unless you take the bus from Nendaz to Siviez - one runs every half hour throughout the day - you have to do some skiing to get home. You can get to the top of Plan du Fou by lift from Tracouet - on the Prarion chairlift, the Fontaines draglift and the Plan du Fou cable car - but once at the top, there is no option but to ski down to Siviez. From Siviez, you can 'lift it' all the way to the top of Lac des Vaux - by the Tortin chairlift and Chassoure-Tortin gondola. Then it's a short ski to the bottom of Lac des Vaux 1, from the top of which you can take a lift all the way home to Verbier - the Funispace followed by a Médran gondola.

savoleyres & la tzoumaz
map p.77

A small, self-contained area, the south side of which you can see from the village. Billed as suitable for intermediates and practising beginners, the blue and red pistes seem less difficult overall than similarly graded pistes elsewhere.

aspect

Savoleyres is an area with two faces and two types of conditions. The south-facing pistes are most susceptible to the sun, and become barer earlier than the pistes in other areas - at the end of the season you can watch the snowline creep upwards on a daily basis. The conditions on the north side stay better for longer.

getting there

to the base station - Verbier's no.1 and no.2 buses go to the Savoleyres lift station. To drive there, follow Route des Creux from the Place Centrale and park in the pay & display on the left side of the station.

up the mountain - the only way up is in the Savoleyres gondola. Although you can see Savoleyres from the slopes of Attelas you can't ski to it from there.

the pistes

blue - surprisingly given its billing, there are no blues from the top of the

---

snapshot

- highest point - 2354m

- aspect - n & s

- lifts - 5 chairs, 1 drag & 2 gondolas

- pistes - 4 blue, 12 red & 1 black

- off-piste - none

- restaurants - 3

Savoleyres gondola. The highest one starts at the top of the Taillay chair - the toboggan run to La Tzoumaz starts here too so watch out for tobogganers heading past.

red - from the top of the Savoleyres gondola red pistes branch off in every direction. On the south face, two wide pistes run down each side of the Savoleyres Sud draglift - the red piste to the left of the lift (as you look down the mountain) is used for competitions and is usually closed to the public. The pistes down to the Tournelle chairlift are also rated red, and are as equally wide and sweeping. On the north side two fairly narrow red pistes run down to the Savoleyres Nord lift and eventually on to La Tzoumaz.

black - the one black here is not always groomed - running just to the right of the top of the Savoleyres Nord chairlift, it cuts across the steep

52

north slope to join the red pistes down to the bottom of this chair.

off-piste

Savoleyres has no official itinerary routes or high mountain tours. However, you will find large areas of ungroomed, and often mogulled, terrain in between the pistes if you want to practise your off-piste technique or bump skiing without venturing too far.

lunch

4 la marmotte
t 027 771 6834

Arguably the best restaurant on the mountain, Marmotte's menu differs from the rest in that along with the usual dishes, it offers *rösti*, served in a variety of ways. Marmotte lies just below the bottom of the Savoleyres Sud drag, so it can be reached on skis - to return to the skiable area you have to brave a lambchop drag. At night, you can reach Marmotte by foot if Route Carrefour is open (a 40 minute walk from Carrefour) or ask the restaurant to send its ski-doo to pick you up. One way to get home is to sledge down to Médran - particularly sensational when there is a full moon.

3 chez simon
t 027 306 8055

A cosy little lunch-spot, there are two small seating areas inside, one downstairs and one tucked upstairs under the eaves. The menu is small but offers some tasty options, including a mushroom *croûte* and the ubiquitous cheese fondue.

1 savoleyres
t 027 771 2116

A huge restaurant with two self-service counters - one on the first floor and the other on the ground floor - open from 11am until 3pm, serving a reasonable selection of hot and cold food. There is also a small coffee bar, which sells filled baguettes for those wanting a quick lunch.

2 sky bar
t 079 449 2916

A snack bar rather than a restaurant, it only opens on sunny days as nearly all the seating is outside. Serving a small selection of sandwiches, waffles and soup, this is a place to grab a drink and watch the paragliders launching from the mountain.

getting home

on skis - there is only one way to ski home at the end of the day - along Route Carrefour, a narrow path through the forest, which joins the blue piste down to Médran. It passes through an avalanche-prone area and so is often closed - check at the top of the Savoleyres whether it is open.

by lift - when Route Carrefour is closed, the only way to get back down to the village is in the Savoleyres gondola.

bruson map p.79

Bruson is probably the prettiest ski area in the 4 Vallées and has not yet fallen victim to the charm of the tourist dollar - the chocolate-box chalets on the tree-lined slopes house locals, not holidaymakers. Totally detached from the rest of the skiing, it is not reachable on skis from Verbier. For this reason it is sometimes forgotten, making it a good place to escape to at weekends or during peak weeks when Verbier's pistes become over-crowded. Other draws are the powder bowls and good tree-skiing. With its overall lower altitude - the highest skiable point is 2200m - on bad weather days whilst the rest of the 4 Vallées suffers from high winds and whirling blizzards, Bruson tends to escape the onslaught. The presence of trees improves the visibility. Often it is the only area open when weather conditions keep the lifts elsewhere closed. More skiers have realised this recently, so now on snowy days although you will be able to ski, you won't be totally alone. A disadvantage of the lower altitude is that in seasons with poor snowfall, Bruson's lower slopes do not get enough cover and because there is no gondola access the whole area has to close.

aspect

Most of the slopes face north-east. When fresh snow falls here it stays powdery for longer so Bruson is often

snapshot

• highest point - 2220m

• aspect - ne & sw

• lifts - 2 chairs & 2 drags

• pistes - 3 blue, 5 red & 1 black

• off-piste - 1 itinerary route

• restaurants - 2

still worth a visit even a few days after a snowfall.

getting there

to the base station - the quickest and most hassle-free way to get to Bruson is by car. Otherwise you have to rely on public transport, which is an efficient service if you time it well. Buses between Le Châble and Bruson run infrequently, with only ten services a day (the first from Le Châble at 8:45am and the last returning from Bruson at 5pm). To get down to Le Châble, take the Médran 2 gondola. When the weather is bad and most of Verbier is trying to get to Bruson the buses are just too small for the quantity of skiers wanting to use them. On these days, either find a friend with a car, or stay in bed.

up the mountain - the only way up the mountain is on the fairly antiquated La Côt chairlift, which starts from the car-park. If you need to buy a lift pass for the area there is a small office at the bottom of this lift.

the pistes
blue - the highest blue is a track from the top of the Pasay chair to the bottom of the Moay drag. It's a pleasant meander through the woods, and unlike other similar tracks is rarely over-crowded. The other blues are also tracks, to the bottom of Bruson or the bottom of Le Châble.

red - the most exciting thing about the reds at Bruson is the change of scenery.

black - the one black piste runs from the top of the Pasay chair. It's a fast descent over a series of lips and rollers.

off-piste
itinerary routes - the descent from the top of the Côt chairlift to Le Châble is an itinerary. It is probably graded as such because it would be impossible to groom - you are skiing through gardens and over fences - and there is only enough coverage a few days each season.

other - for skiers who dream of powder, Bruson's is the most perfect, staying fresh and soft for days. And happily, the pistes cover very little of the area, leaving plenty of bowls and open off-piste areas to explore. Skiing through the trees is also great fun if you can rely on your turns happening

when you want them to. Plan your route carefully, as the forest hides ravines and steep slopes. Tree-skiing is one instance when a helmet can be a life-saver.

lunch
1 côt
t 027 776 1639
A small restaurant serving standard fare. It is rarely busy as it sits on the wrong side of the Côt chairlift, away from the direction of the pistes.

2 moay
t 027 776 1946
A cosy, steamy little place that is as likely to be filled with locals as with skiers. The food is good, and is better value than in other restaurants. Given that you are most likely to be skiing in Bruson when the conditions are less than pleasant, it can seem like an oasis in a snowy desert.

getting home
on skis - as you can't ski from Verbier to Bruson, equally you can't ski the whole way home. But when there has been exceptional snowfall, you can ski to Le Châble. For most of the season though, the bottom of La Côt is as far as you'll get, on either a red or a blue piste.

by lift - none of the lifts are two-directional - there being no gondolas - so once you're up the mountain, the only way down is on skis.

super st. bernard

somewhere else

If you get bored of the 4 Vallées, which you'll be hard pushed to do so, the small ski areas of Champex, La Fouly, Vichères and Super St. Bernard lie within easy reach of Verbier if you have a car. With a Verbier or 4 Vallées lift pass you need only pay a small supplement to ski at any of these areas.

super st. bernard

Of all the satellite areas, the best known is Super St. Bernard. Affectionately known as 'Big Dog', it shares its name with the huge St. Bernard dogs you see lumbering around throughout Valais. It has operated as a ski station since the mid 1960s.

getting there
From Verbier, the journey takes 50 minutes - down through Le Châble, to Sembrancher, where you turn left along the road to the St. Bernard tunnel and Italy. The lift station lies about 7 kms from the village of Bourg St. Pierre, off a turning to the right at the Swiss end of the St. Bernard tunnel.

the skiing
pistes
The pistes in Super St. Bernard run from 2800m to 1900m. On the Swiss side there are two draglifts from which you can ski a short blue run, a

fairly long red, and a black, which often has moguls to rival Tortin's. But the pistes are not the reason most skiers go to Big Dog...

off-piste
...for expert skiers, part of Big Dog's attraction is the off-piste descent into Italy, to the small village of Etrobles in the Val d'Aosta, with the promise of a pasta and Chianti lunch at the bottom - just don't forget to bring your passport.

lunch
There is a small restaurant next to the bottom of the lowest lift on the Swiss side of the mountain. A fairly utilitarian place with little atmosphere, you can at least fill up on calories before venturing out.

getting home
The reverse of getting there.

longer stays
About 6kms from the lift station sits the St. Bernard hospice, which history records as being home to a community of monks for over a thousand years, and a community of St. Bernard dogs for at least a third of that time. A popular stop-over during the summer, in the winter months you can retreat there for a few days if you are willing to brave the elements to reach it - the hospice is not linked by lift and the road is inaccessible during the winter. For reservations call 027 787 1236.

suggested days

So many pistes, so little time. Often it's difficult to know where to start, where to find the longest runs or where to go when there's not much snow or the weather is bad. Here are a few suggestions.

the first morning

lac des vaux - an ideal place to find your ski legs. The area is small and self-contained, with short pistes of varying standards. Even the lifts seem more forgiving - with less of a calf-bashing approach than those in other areas. All pistes end at the bottom of the two lifts - Lac des Vaux 1 and Lac des Vaux 3 - so if your group splits on the way down, you can meet where the lifts begin.

a long day

verbier to thyon - covering about 80kms in one day, this is for intermediate or advanced skiers only. To get there and back without missing any crucial lift links, and to have enough time to explore the many pistes, you need to make an early start. If you want to spend more time around Thyon without worrying about catching the lifts back, you can return to Verbier by road. Taxi is the quickest option as the journey back by public transport takes hours.

The quickest route from Verbier is through Lac des Vaux down Tortin to Siviez and up the Noveli chairlift into Greppon Blanc. The sign to Thyon is easy to miss - where the red pistes split just above the bottom of the Greppon Blanc 3 chair, make sure you take the piste on the right and then a short way down the right fork signposted 'Piste de L'Ours'. The track leads to the Drus drag, which takes you to the top of Thyon, from where you can ski to Mayens de L'Ours, or Veysonnaz, or around Thyon.

When returning to Verbier, the key thing is to leave yourself enough time. There are often long queues at the Chottes draglift in Greppon Blanc, so you need to allow for them. The essential lift links are the Tortin chairlift from Siviez and the Chassoure-Tortin gondola to the top of Lac des Vaux, so check the times of the last lifts on your way to Thyon. However, once you're in Siviez, you're pretty much home and dry - the lifts are timed to ensure that once you are on the Tortin chairlift up from Siviez, you should make the Chassoure-Tortin gondola. The quickest route home is through Lac des Vaux, but if time and energy permits, going via Mont Fort through La Chaux and into Attelas is longer. Lunch is best eaten on your way back through Greppon Blanc.

poor snow conditions

mont fort - two things keep the conditions on Mont Fort better for longer than anywhere else: the glacier, and the high altitude together keep the overall temperature lower so the snow melts at a slower rate. In fact until recently you could ski on the glacier during the summer. When skiing there in the winter, just don't forget to wear your thermals.

bad weather

bruson - as Bruson lies at an overall lower altitude than other areas and is covered by a reasonably dense pine forest, the bad weather never seems quite as bad here. You should still wrap up warm, as all the lifts are uncovered, meaning you're right in the thick of the elements.

a good lunch

chez odette - most of the mountain restaurants in the 4 Vallées are designed to provide sustenance and little else, with a couple of exceptions. Chez Dany just below Ruinettes and Marmotte are old favourites but Chez Odette in Siviez is a little bit special. Odette's does not operate sittings, so you can keep your table as long as you like and peruse the lengthy menu at your leisure. This and the welcome apéritif helps you to feel less like you're on a conveyor belt.

a bumpy ride

tortin, gentianes, mont fort & fontenay - if moguls are your thing, Verbier's slopes are normally covered with them by the middle of the season. A good circular tour is down the itinerary routes of Tortin and

Gentianes, the black piste at Mont Fort and finally the short itinerary route under the Fontenay chair. To start the day more gently, try the route the other way round.

a mid-week change of pace

savoleyres - if after three or four days your enthusiasm for steeps and moguls is starting to wane, a day at Savoleyres can provide the perfect antidote. You have to look hard for any bumps, and most of the pistes are wide and gentle. There are great views in both directions: to the south of the village and down the valley to Grand Combin and on the north side to Nendaz and the Rhone valley. In keeping with a more relaxed day, there are plenty of refreshment stops: the Sky Bar for a mid-morning hot chocolate, Marmotte for a long, leisurely lunch in an authentic setting and a vin chaud at Carrefour at the end of Route Carrefour to round off the day.

après

chez dany - situated on the sunny plateau of Clambin, there is nowhere better up the mountain from where to enjoy the end of the skiing day. True it's rarely quiet, but Dany's is a dab hand at dealing with the crowds and you never wait long to be served. The only thing to remember is that you've still got a bit of skiing to do before you're home.

off-piste

For many, off-piste is where the real skiing starts. And Verbier is a good place to look for reality, as testified to by the long snakes of keen boarders and skiers trekking up steep couloirs or making exhausting traverses to find the holy grail.

Verbier's off-piste has two personalities. The itinerary routes and high mountain tours are the gentler side and see skiers and boarders of varying standards skiing or tumbling down them whilst the ungroomed and unmapped back-country is rougher, tougher and makes greater demands on technique.

itinerary routes
Until recently Tortin and Gentianes were groomed and classified as blacks. Certainly the traffic that uses them each day can make them appear piste-like. They can be skied without a guide, but as conditions are variable they should not be undertaken lightly.

high mountain tours
Generally harder than the itinerary routes, they tend to see fewer skiers, which makes the descents less obvious. This is just one reason to ski them with a guide.

other off-piste
It would take a whole book to describe the extent of the back-country with justice. The starting point for much of the off-piste is Mont Fort and routes from here can take you as far as Fionnay or in the other direction past Lac de Cleuson to Siviez. On the south side of Bruson, when conditions permit, you can ski off-piste all the way to Sembrancher or Orsières. Whilst none of the off-piste runs are as well known as the Vallée Blanche in nearby Chamonix, the main attraction is that most of them are easily reached from the main lifts and ski area, though you may first need to traverse a slope or ascend a couloir. The effort put in to get there only heightens the experience further, and increases the reward.

Perhaps contrary to what you might think, intermediate skiers will find something to suit them. Verbier's off-piste skiing isn't just about vertical drops and narrow couloirs and some routes are gently-sloped bowls with flatteringly do-able descents, the perfect starting place for powder virgins. The best way to enjoy the off-piste fully and safely is with a guide - see **mountain guides**. If you ski off-piste without one you do so at your own risk. You should always take the right equipment with you - an avalanche transceiver, a shovel and a probe - and you should always pay attention to the avalanche and safety signs and warnings. Never go on your own and make sure your insurance covers off-piste skiing.

ski touring

A whole world of skiing goes almost unnoticed by most recreational skiers - those used to huge, well linked ski areas and mile after mile of pistes may not know what ski touring is. Also known as ski mountaineering, perhaps a more appropriate name, you climb up the mountains without using the lifts before skiing down. Touring is entirely off-piste and on a 'tour' you travel from 'a' to 'b' in the same way as hiking up mountains in summer.

60

Obviously, different equipment is necessary. To climb up slopes you need skis with touring bindings, which unlock to allow the heel to come away from the ski as you step upwards. You also carry 'skins' - now artificial but so called because they were originally seal skins - to attach to the base of the skis during a climb to prevent them from slipping down. Whilst some don't see the logic in ignoring an efficient lift system, little compares to the satisfaction felt after a physically demanding ascent or descent as well as the enjoyment of being amidst the alpine scenery, away from the mêlée of the pistes.

touring in verbier
If you want to learn the techniques for touring, all of the ski schools offer lessons. Once you have mastered the basics, by far the best - and safest - way to explore further is with a guide.

Verbier's off-piste offers too many tours to mention here, except for the impossible to ignore Verbier to Zermatt *haute route*. As with all off-piste skiing, you should never go alone, always wear an avalanche transceiver and carry a probe and a shovel. Also inform someone of your itinerary and likely time of return.

Ski touring is possible throughout the whole season, but March and April are when it comes into its own, as the weather is more predictable and the days are longer.

the haute route
The original, classic *haute route* (high level road) first skied in the early 20th century, runs between Chamonix and Zermatt. You can join the route from Verbier, going in either direction, although the route to Zermatt is regarded as more stunning and less tiring. The whole tour takes 6 or 7 days and you normally join the classic route on the 3rd or 4th day. It makes real demands on your skiing and your personal fitness, and it should not be undertaken without considerable preparation and a guide. The ski schools often run *haute route* tours, or you can go with an independent guide or one of the guiding companies based in Verbier - see the **directory**. Your reward is an exhilirating journey in some of the most beautiful mountain scenery in the world, from Mont Fort to the Matterhorn.

events

Verbier isn't a stop on the skiing World Championships timetable - but it hosts plenty of other events during the season. The dates change yearly, so check with the tourist office or on the relevant website.

24 hour freeride

The events season kicks off in mid-December when skiers compete in the 24 hour freeride, an event to raise money to benefit the victims of anti-personnel mines. Teams of four compete against the clock, attempting to ski the designated route as many times as they can.

verbier ride

There is not much in the events calendar until March and the Verbier Ride, started in 1999 by Warren Smith. The world's elite free-style skiers meet to show off their skills in 3 disciplines. In the Big Mountain Freeride skiers hurtle down Mont Gelé at break-neck speed. In the SkierX, groups of four skiers compete head-to-head on a specially designed course of slalom gates, banked turns, moguls and rollers. The Big Air allows individuals to wow the crowds with their impressive jumps in the Snowpark at La Chaux. For more details see verbierride.ch

o'neill xtreme

A 3 day invitation-only competition of 25 of the world's best male and female boarders. Held on the north face of the Bec des Rosses, marks are awarded for speed, style and difficulty of line. The best spot to watch the death-defying descents is the Col des Gentianes restaurant. Coverage is also shown on the specially installed screens on Rue de Médran, which also show extreme skiing and boarding videos during the event. This compliments the street-party atmosphere in the resort - live bands competing for an audience and stalls selling vin chaud and t-shirts.

swiss downhill championship

A leg of the Mens and Womens Swiss Downhill is held in March on the black piste from the top of the Funispace to the bottom of Combe 1. A fairly low-key event, it is mainly of interest to the Swiss, but it's one way to get close to Ski Sunday speeds.

carlsberg high five & verbier challenge cup

The end of the season sees two smaller events open to amateurs in all disciplines. The first is the Carlsberg High Five, 5 competitions - giant slalom, skierX, boarderX, cross-country and a 'triathlon'- in one. The second is the Challenge Cup, a giant slalom run by the Ski Club of Great Britain. All levels are welcome and you register in the class suitable to your age and ability. For both, more information is displayed on posters around the village.

snow activities

It's not all down, down, down - here are a few ideas for something else to do on the snow. All contact details are listed in the **directory**.

cross-country skiing

If you intend to spend every day of your holiday in Verbier on cross-country skis, you will soon get bored. But for a few hours or a day there are four routes within easy reach. In Verbier itself, a 5km trail runs from Ruinettes to La Chaux and a 4km trail circles the Verbier Centre Sportif. Further afield, a 20km circular trail starts and ends in Le Châble and a 5 km circular trail runs around Lourtier. A map of the trails is available from the tourist office.

heliskiing

Think hard before you book your first heliskiing trip, as for many there is no going back to skiing on-piste. Equally don't get too despondent if you don't go when planned - helicopter travel is particularly susceptible to changes in the weather.

Heliskiing isn't legal in nearby France, so business booms in Verbier. The most popular destinations are Rosablanche (3314m), Petit Combin (3670m) or on the Trient glacier (3295m). The helicopter lands before you start to ski - much to the dis-appointment of any would-be action heroes - and you are then led by a guide through snow that is almost guaranteed to be track-free. Maison du Sport and La Fantastique will organise heliskiing (with guides) for you, or you can book directly with Air Glaciers.

night-skiing

Maison du Sport organises weekly night-skiing at Les Esserts. Aimed mainly at children, it's a short descent on the nursery slope. Despite being apparently easy, the piste is a very different creature at night - see how good your technique is when you can't quite see all the bumps...

tobogganing

On Attelas a 7km route runs from Ruinettes to Verbier and on Savoleyres a 10km run starts at the top of the Taillay chair down through the forest to Tzoumaz. Tobogganners can also use Route Carrefour, when it is open, from Savoleyres to Carrefour and from there join the toboggan run down from Ruinettes at the bottom of the Mayentzet chairlift. You can rent toboggans from most ski shops for between CHF8 to CHF15 per day.

snowshoeing

For those who can't or don't want to don skis, this is an excellent way to enjoy the scenery. Equipment has been modernised a bit, but you still effectively wear tennis rackets to tramp around the mountains. You can book a guide through Maison du Sport or La Fantastique.

copyright winter press 2003

67

lac des vaux, attelas & la chaux

key on inside back cover

lift	time	information
mont fort 100	4m10s	**pistes** steep **bumps** long, steep **queues** occasional, slow-moving **off-piste** extensive, varied, steep, open, couloirs, bowls **other** often closes during snowfall or in high winds
jumbo 150	6m05s	**pistes** narrow **queues** rare, fast-moving **other** closes during snowfall or in high winds, see below
glacier 1/2 ②	————	**pistes** wide **other** only 1 drag is usually open, gentianes itinerary route starts at the bottom of these lifts.
les gentianes ②	————	**other** rarely open
col des gentianes 125	7m35s	**pistes** varied **queues** common, slow-moving, see below
chassoure-tortin ⑧	7m45s	**bumps** long, steep **off-piste** extensive, open **queues** frequent, peak times, up to 20 mins **other** lac des vaux access, see below

At col des gentianes expect to wait at least 10 minutes between the arrival of the lift and its next departure. To reach ④ take the red piste at the top of the jumbo back down to la chaux. To reach the 4 vallées without skiing the tortin itinerary, descend in the chassoure-tortin gondola.

1 la chotte de tortin
2 cabane du tortin
3 col des gentianes
4 cabane du mont fort

key on inside back cover

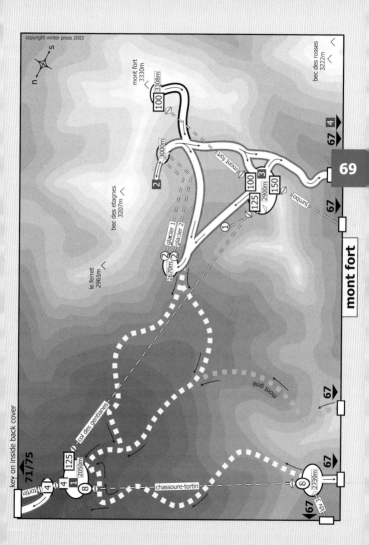

key on inside back cover

mont fort

69

67 4

67

67

67

71/75

tortin

mont fort 3330m

bec des rosses 3222m

bec des etagnes 3207m

le ferret 2965m

mont fort 3308m

100

3000m 2

2

2 glacier 1
2 glacier 2
2670m

125 2900m 100 3
150

jumbo

1

mont gelé

col des gentianes

2050m
125
4
1
8

chassoure-tortin

2739m
8

KW 3

siviez & greppon blanc

lift	time	information
tortin |4| - from siviez	9m55s	**queues** common, afternoon **other** verbier access, see below
- from tortin	1m40s	**other** access to the top of the blue piste down to siviez
novelij |2|	12m00s	**pistes** long, wide **queues** common, slow-moving, peak times
greppon blanc 1 ①	6m55s	**pistes** track initially **queues** common, peak times **off-piste** moderate, varied **other** thyon and veysonnaz access
greppon blanc 2 ①	6m30s	**pistes** steep **queues** common, peak times **other** verbier and nendaz access, see below
greppon blanc 3 |2|	5m30s	**pistes** steep **queues** rare **off-piste** moderate, varied
meina ①	6m20s	**pistes** long, wide **queues** rare
chottes ②	5m45s	**pistes** long, wide **queues** common, lunch - afternoon, peak times
tsa ②	3m05s	**queues** rare **other** greppon blanc access from thyon

When returning to verbier on greppon blanc 2 you can come off halfway up the lift if you are short of time. The return journey from siviez to the tortin mid-station on tortin can be very cold in the afternoon.

1 combatzeline
2 aux chottes
3 chez odette

key on inside back cover

70

siviez & greppon blanc

71

key on inside back cover

thyon, mayen de l'ours & veysonnaz

lift	time	information
etherolla |2|	12m05s	**pistes** long, steep **queues** rare **other** greppon blanc access
les masses|2|	12m00s	**queues** occasional, morning
from mid-station	7m00s	
muraz ②		**pistes** gentle, wide
theytaz 2 ②		**pistes** gentle, wide
trabanta |4|		**pistes** gentle, wide **queues** occasional, morning
joc ②		**other** use to get up the mountain if queues for trabanta
theytaz 1 ①		**pistes** gentle, wide
matze ②		**pistes** gentle, wide
les crêtes ②		**pistes** long, narrow **other** greppon blanc access
cheminée ②	5m15s	**pistes** long, narrow **other** greppon blanc access
piste de l'ours ④	9m15s	**pistes** long, wide, slushy at bottom **queues** occasional, morning
combyre ②		**other** sometimes closed
drus ②		**other** link from greppon blanc to thyon
veysonnaz ④	15m00s	**pistes** long, wide, slushy at bottom **queues** occasional, morning

1 mont rouge

thyon, mayen de l'ours & veysonnaz

73

copyright winter press 2003

key on inside back cover

mont carré
2549m

2453m

2413m

71

2163m 2 tsei

2370m

2 crêtes

2 cheminée

2220m

etherolla
2

1874m
2

les masses

muraz
1910m 2

2190m

theytaz 2

1930m

1915m

2160m

1

trabanta

2120m

srup
2 1975m

1800m
4

1850m
joc
2 1

2

2065m

1

1

1

4

4

inalpe
1

2030m

thyon
2000m

theytaz 1

1860m
2 1

matze

piste de l'ours gondola

mayen de l'ours

veysonnaz gondola

combyre gondola

veysonnaz

2610m
2

lift	time	information
siviez 2	7m20s	**queues** rare **other** closed in poor conditions, see below
plan du fou ②	7m00s	**queues** rare
plan du fou 60	5m30s	**bumps** short, steep **off-piste** moderate, open **queues** rare
les fontaines ②	6m00s	**pistes** steep, icy, often bare and rocky
prarion 4	7m10s	**pistes** varied **other** lift is two-directional between tracouet and the bottom of les fontaines
jean-pierre ②		**pistes** varied **off-piste** moderate, trees
pracondu 1 ②		**other** often closed in poor conditions
tracouet 12	12m30s	**pistes** varied **queues** common, peak times
alpage ②		**queues** rare
dent ①		**queues** rare
lac ①		**pistes** gentle **queues** rare

When siviez is closed, the only way to access the skiing in nendaz is to take the bus from siviez to nendaz village.

1 plan du fou
2 tracouet
3 chez odette

copyright winter press 2003

69

71

71

novelli

siviez 1730m

tortin

siviez

2185m

2235m

mont gond 2667m

plan du fou 2438m

plan du fou **100**

100 2140m

les fontaines

pointe de balavaux 2456m

dent de nendaz 2463m

1839m

prarion

nendaz

2170m

lac

2226m

dent

2170m

2200m

jean-pierre

2112m

alpage 1896m

tracouet gondola

pracondu 1670m

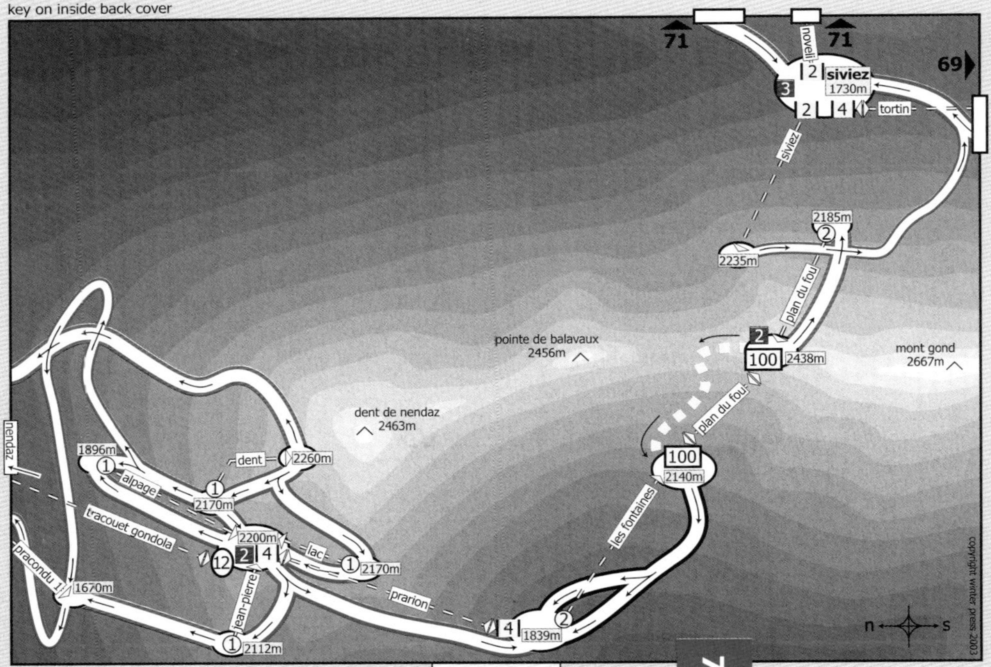

nendaz

savoleyres & la tzoumaz

lift	time	information
savoleyres gondola ④	14m05s	**pistes** varied **queues** occasional, peak times **other** use to get home when route carrefour is closed, see below
tournelle |2|		**pistes** wide **queues** occasional, peak times
savoleyres sud ①		**pistes** long, wide **other** lift starts at mid-way point in poor snow
savoleyres nord |6|	4m11s	**pistes** long **bumps** varied **off-piste** open, varied **queues** rare **other** see below
taillay |4|		**pistes** wide, gentle **queues** common, peak times
les etablons |2|		**queues** rare
la tzoumaz gondola ④	15m00s	**pistes** varied **queues** common, peak times **other** see below
tzoumaz |2|		**other** closed in poor conditions

At the end of the day the journey back up on savoleyres nord can be cold. The journey on the savoleyres gondola and la tzoumaz gondola can be slow because of age of lifts and loading of toboggans.

1 savoleyres
2 sky bar
3 chez simon
4 la marmotte

key on inside back cover

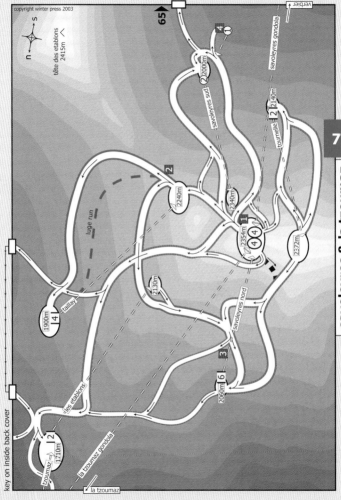

savoleyres & la tzoumaz

key on inside back cover

tête des etablons
2415m

65

verbier

savoleyres gondola

2140m

tournelle 2

savoleyres sud

2200m 2

4 1

2354m 1

4 4

2372m

2240m 2

2340m

luge run

2130m

savoleyres nord

1900m 4

taillay

3

2060m 6

les etablons

la tzoumaz gondola

tzoumaz 2

1710m

la tzoumaz

bruson

lift	time	information
la côt │2│	8m30s	**pistes** varied, slushy **off-piste** limited, trees **queues** occasional, morning **other** closed when snow does not reach village level, see below
moay ②	5m00s	**pistes** narrow, slushy **queues** rare
la pasay │3│	7m15s	**pistes** varied **off-piste** extensive, trees **queues** rare
grand-tsai ②	5m40s	**pistes** varied **off-piste** extensive, varied, bowls, open, trees **queues** rare

When │la côt│ is closed, the whole area is closed as none of the lifts are two-directional.

│1│ la côt
│2│ moay

key on inside back cover

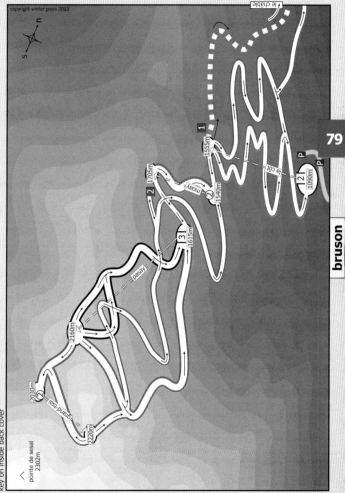

key on inside back cover

79

bruson

le châble

pointe de sesal
2302m

grand-tsai 2030m

2220m

2160m

pasay

2 1705m

3 1615m

moay-s

1540m

1 1555m

la côt

2 1090m

P P

the resort

food & drink

Cheese, cheese everywhere, and nothing else to eat? Those fearing that the choice will be fondue, fondue or more fondue will be pleasantly surprised. Such is the range of eateries, it's almost impossible to categorise them - pretty much every popular form of cuisine is represented. In addition to local dishes and the ubiquitous fondue you can eat sushi, curry, haute cuisine, pizza and burgers. And if you want to eat up the mountain, both Chez Dany (see **les attelas**) and La Marmotte (see **savoleyres & la tzoumaz**) open for dinner if there is sufficient demand.

82

restaurants

The reviews are split into 'local' restaurants, being those which serve food typical to the Valais region, and 'general', which is everything else.

useful information

bars - most of the restaurants reviewed have a small bar where you can have a quick drink before dinner.

hotels - some of the resort's hotels have a restaurant, open to non-residents. The best are mentioned in the relevant hotel review.

reservations - demand for seats is high, so at weekends and during peak weeks reservations for evening dining

---

snapshot

for something...
- at breakfast - offshore
- cheap - chez martin
- cheesy - le caveau
- expensive - roland pierroz
- from après to evening - le fer à cheval
- late - harold's hamburgers
- meaty - el toro negro
- naughty but nice - the milk bar
- romantic - le bouchon gourmand
- with a view - sonalon

---

are essential, particularly for larger groups.

sittings - most restaurants run two-sittings one at 7pm and one at 9pm.

terraces - with so many sunny days, most restaurants find space for a terrace. As temperatures fall at night they are open only during the day.

prices
Either because you're dining up a mountain, or simply because it's Switzerland, eating out is not a cheap experience. In the reviews the grading (1)-(5) reflects the price per head for a main course excluding drinks.
(1) below CHF10
(2) CHF10-20
(3) CHF20-30
(4) CHF30-40
(5) above CHF40
Unless otherwise stated, all reviewed restaurants accept most credit cards.

au vieux verbier (4)

map - town f/g4
t 027 771 1668
open 11:30am-11:30pm
food traditional swiss
terrace ✓

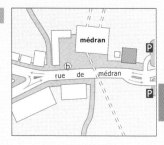

A deservedly popular venue for lunch, après or dinner, and conveniently located next to the Médran lift station. Au vieux Verbier is a large family-run restaurant - the inside seats up to 150 people - on the ground floor of the hotel of the same name. Despite its size, the traditional alpine style gives it a special charm, service is genteel and you will always receive a warm welcome.

Lunch is served from midday until 3.30pm, and in good weather the spacious terrace opens to allow you to idle away your afternoon in the sunshine with a special afternoon tea menu - or something stronger.

The dinner service starts at 7pm but those looking for fondue should look elsewhere - au vieux Verbier is proud not to serve it. Instead, the house speciality, *La Potence* (the gallows) is highly recommended. Chunks of good-quality beef hung on a spiky metal frame are flambéed at the table and served with a rich bourguignon sauce, rice and tasty French fries. Another house speciality is pan-fried perch from Lake Geneva, which is similarly delicious.

« local »

le caveau (3)

map - town c2
t 027 771 2226
open 12pm-11:30pm
food fondue & raclette
terrace ✓ (on sunny days)

84

The place in Verbier for fondue - choose from classic cheese, meat, or tomato served with potatoes. Raclette is also a speciality. Justifiably popular for the delicious food and pleasant atmosphere, on most nights you need to reserve a table, although the earnest maître d' always makes an effort to find space. Those who have had their fill of the local dishes can choose from a wide selection of very generous and tasty salads, spatchcock chicken or steak. If you have room for dessert, the choice is limited to ice-cream and sorbet - but few can manage more.

le carrefour (3)

map - valley d6
t 027 771 7010/5555

open 10am-10:30pm
food traditional swiss
terrace ✓

A convenient place for skiers and non-skiers to meet for lunch, Carrefour is located at the end of bus route 1 and can be reached from both Attelas and Savoleyres on skis. It is also good for a relaxed meal in the evening, if you have a car or can afford a taxi. The house speciality is the 'hot stone' - you cook your choice of meat (beef, pork or ostrich) at your table on a sizzling hot plate. Served with a salad and rösti - the owner's trademark - it is simple, but delicious.

marlenaz (4)

map - valley a6
t 027 771 5441
open during the day when sunny
food traditional swiss
terrace ✓

Tucked away in the forest on the Savoleyres side, Marlenaz is not easy to get to, but is worth the effort. A perfect lunch spot on a sunny day, the terrace faces up the valley with a fantastic view of Grand Combin. During the winter, there is no access by road and the only way there is on foot - a 20 minute walk up the dirt track from Sonalon. The menu offers a tasty selection of local dishes and the day's special is often a good choice.

le sonalon (4)

map - valley b6
t 027 771 7271
open 12pm-2:30pm, 6:30pm-11pm
food traditional swiss
terrace ✓

A perennial favourite with locals and visitors alike, Sonalon is deservedly popular for lunch and dinner. Situated on the Savoleyres side, it is closer to the village than Marlenaz - but unless you can face the long uphill walk, the best way there is by car. When the sun shines, the large sun-trap of a terrace is a big attraction. The vast menu will also hold your attention. Sonalon's one drawback? As its sits beneath the Savoleyres gondola, you may feel a twinge of guilt that you are eating lunch rather then skiing.

snapshot

does it come with chips?
For those who have never tried it (and even those who have), the attraction of a **fondue** may be difficult to understand - the dish is an artery-blocking blend of cheese (typically gruyère), white wine, garlic and kirsch, in which you dip pieces of nearly stale bread. Dr Atkins wouldn't approve, but it's a delicious combination.

The appeal of **raclette**, a Valaisian speciality, is as equally confusing for anybody who watches their health or their calorie intake. A half-moon of Bagnes cheese is heated until the top edge is soft, and the cheese is then scraped off and served with potatoes. Little beats it when the blizzard is raging and skiing is low down on the list of priorities.

It being Switzerland, you might expect **rösti** (a fried, grated potato cake) to be on every menu. Not so in Verbier - the local cuisine is influenced by French rather than German cooking. Where rösti is served (Marmotte and Carrefour), it is a less dense dish than you find in resorts further east. What you will see on menus is a **croûte**. Made of layers of bread and cheese, soaked in wine and with layers of ham or mushrooms if you wish, it is then baked in the oven and served piping hot - and is very filling and tasty.

85

« general »

al capone (2)

86

map - valley c5
t 027 771 6774
open 11:30am-11:30pm
food pizza & pasta
terrace ×

Halfway between Savoleyres and the Place Centrale along Route des Creux, Al Capone is one of the few restaurants in the heart of Verbier's chalet-land. So if you don't want to wander too far when your chalet girl has her night off, it's a low-key, cheapish place to go with reasonable pizzas and a relaxed atmosphere. As most chalet staff have the same night off, you should make sure you book a table.

alpage (3)

map - town b1
t 027 771 6121
open 6:30pm-11pm
food swiss-italian
terrace ×

Traditional mountain food and style with a modern twist. New in 2003, the

Alpage lies on the ground floor of the Hotel Rhodania. Tastefully decorated throughout, pictures of *olde Verbiere* hang from rough, cream-coloured walls and the wooden furniture is covered with cow-hide throws. On dark, snowy evenings, the candle-lit room feels cosy. Food is rustic and hearty and served in quite generous portions. Service can be erratic, but is always friendly.

borsalino pizzeria (2)

map - town c3
t 027 771 1750
open 11:30am-11:30pm
food pizza & pasta
terrace ×

The finest Italian job in Verbier. The pizza - baked in a wood-fired oven, with a thin, crispy base and interesting toppings - is the best in the resort, and the homemade pasta and steak is also good. With its bustling but relaxed atmosphere it is a great place for families or large groups, and you don't have to keep an eye on the noise levels. You're unlikely to get a table without reservation but if you are a small group and there are no tables you may be able to eat at the bar.

le bouchon gourmand (3)

map - town b2
t 027 771 7296
open 12pm-10:30pm
food french provençal
terrace ✓ (small)

You could be forgiven for thinking you're in Provence - the décor does a great impression of a bistro in south-west France. And the tasty food will convince you further - all dishes are French Provençal and include foie gras and magret de canard. With its cosy and intimate atmosphere, Le Bouchon is a good spot for couples seeking romance or somewhere quiet for a clandestine rendez-vous.

chez kamal (2)

map - town a1
t 027 771 7628
open 11:30am-11pm
food indian/indonesian
terrace ×

The only place in Verbier to indulge your craving for chicken tikka masala. Although it doesn't rival most local Tandooris in England, the food at least offers something different. A mixture of Indian and Indonesian - the décor is the same - the menu includes favourites like chicken korma and nasi goreng. A buffet is served on Friday and Saturday evenings - all you can eat for CHF15 from a selection of meat and vegetable dishes, served - of course - with popadoms.

chez martin (2)

map - town b/c1
t 027 771 2252
open 11:30am-11pm
food pizza & pasta
terrace ×

Verbier's cheapest restaurant, Chez Martin serves up standard fare pizza and pasta in a large, fairly bland room.

The lunch menu, available 11.30am-2pm, is good value - two courses cost CHF15 and there are six set menus. Families and big groups shouldn't struggle to get a table and it's one choice for those searching for food outside normal mealtimes.

el toro negro (4)

map - town c3
t 027 771 9901
open 6:30pm-11pm
food steak
terrace ×

Not a restaurant for vegetarians, El Toro Negro's business is in meat: good-quality beef, ostrich or pork. Portions are huge, so although the extensive salad bar looks - and is - delicious make sure you leave room for your main course. Reservations are essential and when you book, clearly state you want a table at El Toro Negro, as the restaurant shares its booking line with Le Millennium. Can be booked for private parties.

le fer à cheval (3)

map - town e3
t 027 771 2669
open 9:30am-11:30pm
food pizza, pasta & brasserie
terrace ✓

Known affectionately as the 'Furry' or the 'Shovel', the giant iron horse-shoe on the roof makes this bar/restaurant hard to miss. Better known for its après in the afternoon, from 7pm the Furry turns into a full-blown restaurant

87

offering pizzas, tasty salads and grilled meats. Whilst the food would disappoint connoisseurs, people love the lively atmosphere and friendly service and it's one of the few places in Verbier where you can order food after 10pm. As it's very popular make sure you book.

88 le millennium (3)

map - town c3
t 027 771 9900
open 9am-12am
food international
terrace ✓ (small)

Although Le Millennium has the same owner as El Toro Negro, the choice isn't limited to steak - it is one of the few places to serve a selection of fish, seafood and vegetarian dishes. But you need strong muscles to lift the heavy metal-bound menu, stamina to choose from the seemingly endless selection of dishes and dedication to finish the huge portions.

netsu (3)

map - town d3
t 027 771 6272
open 6:30pm-11pm (not mondays)
food sushi
terrace ×

If something seems wrong about sushi at high altitude in a land-locked country, Netsu makes it right. It's difficult to fault the attention to detail - nothing is missing from the Japanese theme. You can eat the good, fresh sushi and sashimi at high chairs at the bar - ideal for lone diners - or the more sociable long, black tables and wash it down with sake or just a beer.

la pinte (3/4)

map - town e3
t 027 771 6323
open 6:30pm-11pm
food french
terrace ×

With its ice-laden trolleys of fresh seafood and bustling, open-fronted kitchen, La Pinte would fit in well on the Champs Elysées. But once at your table the atmosphere is more typically Swiss. Tablecloths are snow-white, wine glasses twinkle and the service is attentive and friendly. The cooking is supervised by Roland Pierroz (see below), with the result that the food is uncomplicated and excellent.

roland pierroz (5)

map - town e3
t 027 771 6323
open 12pm-11pm
food haute cuisine
terrace ✓ (small)

The only restaurant in Verbier with a Michelin star - and a price bracket to match. Verbier's king of cuisine, Roland Pierroz, has presided over the cooking at his name-sake restaurant for over 20 years. Food and wine vie for first place, but receive equally careful treatment - the cellar contains some 50,000 different bottles and the food would compete with that served in top London eateries.

cafés

A skiing holiday is the one time you can feel justified in indulging in something highly calorific. As you would expect, the boulangeries dotted around town are filled with tempting tarts and cakes if your sweet tooth needs instant gratification. For treats at a more leisurely pace there are plenty of places to stop. Most of the cafés and tea-rooms open for breakfast, and stay open all day to serve lunch and - of course - afternoon tea. If you pay a visit to Verbier-village, the Marienda tea-room at the back of the Michellod bakery is a good place to stop for refreshment.

milk bar (1)

map - town c/d2
t 027 771 6777
open 8am-7pm
food tarts & cakes
terrace ✓

The Milk Bar does a startlingly good impression of a Cotswold tea-shop, with its chintzy décor, black and white clad waitresses and dark wood furnishings. However, the delicious fresh tarts and cakes are more French pâtisserie than Stow-on-the-Wold. For drinks, the hot chocolate and thick, ice-cream based milkshakes are recommended. With its politely quiet atmosphere it's a comfortable place to spend some time with a newspaper, or to hide from the bad weather when a blizzard howls outside.

le monde des crêpes (1)

map - town b2
t 027 771 2895
open 11am-7pm
food crêpes
terrace ✓ (small)

It wouldn't be a ski resort if there wasn't a crêperie - and Le Monde on Rue de la Poste is the only one. You can choose from a wide range of savoury and sweet filings - including mushrooms, cheese or ham, and chocolate or classic sugar and lemon - to eat there or on the move.

89

offshore (2)

map - town f4
t 027 771 5444
open 8am-7pm
food burgers & tex-mex
terrace ✓ (small)

More inland than offshore, you probably wouldn't expect to find a surf shack in the mountains. Decked out with surf boards, a pink VW Beetle and waikiki prints, it can feel a bit surreal when every inch of your skin is covered in thermal clothing. But Offshore deservedly pulls in the punters for its burgers, tex-mex and ribs. More of a diner than a café, it also serves a brunch menu (until 11.30am) for late-risers who miss breakfast. Service is lethargic, but if you position yourself near one of the TVs showing extreme skiing, boarding and surfing videos, you probably won't notice. The main gripe? Offshore is closed in the evening.

late night

For some reason most of Verbier's restauranteurs think hunger stops at 10pm. Only two places are open for midnight feasters.

harold's hamburgers (2)

90

map - town c2
t 027 771 6243
open 10am-1:30am
food hamburgers
terrace ×

Famous for uncommunicative and unfriendly service of which Harold's seems proud - the inside displays even less than glowing reviews. Food is average and over-priced, but as Offshore closes at 7pm, Harold's is the only place you can get a burger in the evening. A plus point for some is that you can check your emails while you eat - see the **directory**.

the bakery (1)

map - town b/c2
open from 2am
food croissants
terrace ×

Got a craving for a midnight kebab? Well, Verbier can't deliver there. However, the bakery on Rue de Verbier has an alternative answer to the late-night munchies. On the way back from the Farm, it's difficult to ignore the aroma from the kitchen, and you will be drawn to a small window where CHF2 rewards you with a pain au chocolat fresh from the oven.

take-away

If you are staying in and can't be bothered to cook, a few places will let you take-away, although only one delivers. For a ski resort the choice isn't bad - pizza from **borsalino**, **chez martin** or **le fer à cheval**, curry or Indonesian from **chez kamal**, crêpes from **le monde des crêpes** or sushi from **sushi-switzerland**, who deliver (**t** 079 510 8920) - and it at least means there's no washing-up to do.

For a cheap and quick lunch on the hoof, the choice is more limited. As the supermarkets and bakeries close for their own lunch from 12.30pm to 3pm, you can have sandwiches, or sandwiches. From **offshore** you can get generously stuffed and tasty baguettes with your choice of fillings. Or the small *buvette* next to the TéléVerbier lift pass booth at Médran sells sandwiches and pastries from the Michellod bakery. You can also take-away hot and cold drinks and other snacks.

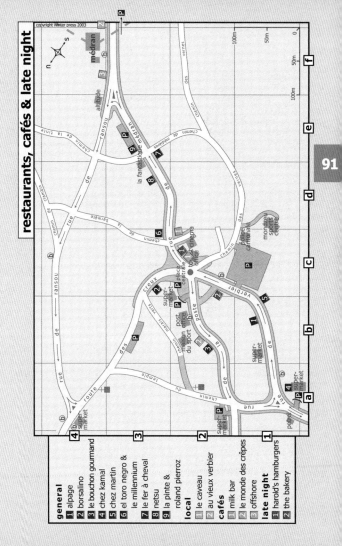

restaurants, cafés & late night

copyright winter press 2003

91

general

4
1 alpage
2 borsalino
3 le bouchon gourmand
4 chez kamal
5 chez martin
6 el toro negro &
  le millennium
3
7 le fer à cheval
8 netsu
9 la pinte &
  roland pierroz

local
2
1 le caveau
2 au vieux verbier

cafés
1 milk bar
2 le monde des crêpes
3 offshore

late night
1
1 harold's hamburgers
2 the bakery

après-ski & nightlife

For those with any energy left, the
après-ski and nightlife has something
to suit all tastes - an après-ski
sharpener, a quiet drink in the pub, or
cocktails and dancing later. Apart
from a couple of places, the vibe is
casual and relaxed. Après-ski is
similar to what you find in other
resorts - by late afternoon the
bars and pubs fill with red-faced
skiers seeking to recount the tales of
the day over a few beers. Most
disappear from 7pm for dinner in
their chalets or one of the many
restaurants. The nightlife proper kicks
off at 10pm and ends as late (or
early) as 4am, for those able to stay
awake that long.

bars & pubs

Most of the bars are run and staffed
by English-speaking ex-pats and
seasonnaires.

useful information
hotel bars - many of the hotels have
bars, which welcome non-residents as
well as guests. Opening times
fluctuate, the bar generally staying
open until the last drinker leaves.

liveliness - Tuesdays, Thursdays and
Sundays are the popular nights out
amongst the seasonnaire population,
and places like the Pub Mont Fort and
Murphy's Bar - and later - Tara's teem
with partying chalet staff. On other

> ### snapshot
>
> **après...**
> - classic après - le fer à cheval
> - happy hour - pub mont fort
> - sing-along - hotel farinet
>
> **après après...**
> - cocktails - king's bar
> - happy seasonnaires - pub mont fort
> - swiss chic - crok no name
>
> **& dawn-breakers**
> - beautiful people - the farm
> - just for fun - tara's
> - techno-tastic - marshal's

nights, a lot of the bars can be
subdued, unless they are hosting a
pub crawl or pub quiz for a UK tour
operator. Weekends are busier, when
weekenders flood in.

on the slopes - the après scene is
very much centred in the village. Only
Chez Dany and Carrefour on the
mountain are open for après and
even then you don't find the same
dancing on tables approach that is
popular in some Austrian resorts.

prices
Liquid refreshment doesn't come
cheap no matter where you go - a
spirit and mixer costs around CHF10,
and a cocktail CHF15. Beer is the
cheapest at about CHF5 for a half
litre. And as anywhere, buying wine
by the bottle is more cost effective -
as long as you can drink it all.

bars & pubs

crok no name
map - town b3
t 027 771 6934
open 6.30pm-1am
food ×
tv ×

An oasis of calm compared with the other more typical ski resort bars, Crok No Name is unaffectedly chic and cool. The décor is an eclectic mix of styles - the tinfoil-esque ceiling makes you think of Buck Rodgers, whilst for seats you can choose between a lipstick-red sofa, a fluffy two-seater, a chair made from antlers or some high-legged metal stools. Somehow, it works, and you could almost be convinced that you are in a bar of a more bohemian part of a European city rather than a ski resort.

Mid-week, the atmosphere can be subdued, perhaps because the prices are too high for most punters. Things rarely get started before 11pm, so even if you want to guarantee yourself a table and seats, you can take your time about getting there. At weekends, the black-clad Geneva set move in pre Farm Club, to enjoy the cocktails and the DJ's choice of Café del Mar inspired tracks.

For drinks, the usual wines and beer are served, but if you want to splash out go for the speciality cocktail - a dangerous blend of a long island iced tea and a margarita called a Royal. Expensive, but one should be enough.

« bars & pubs »

big ben

map - town e3
t 027 771 1050
open 11am-1pm
food ✓ (bar snacks)
   tv ✗

94

No explanation is given for the name, but no big clocks are visible. Big Ben is popular for après, perhaps because it's the first drinks stop after Médran. You can enjoy the late afternoon rays from one of the benches crowded on the small terrace at the front. In the evening, the crowd is younger, probably attracted by the five pool tables, video games and table football.

hotel farinet

map - town c3
t 027 771 6626
open 10am-1pm
food 4pm-10am (bar snacks)
tv ✓

If Mother Brown skied, this is where she would knees-up. Two venues in one, you can opt for riotous fun or relaxed calm. Every day as the slopes empty, the glass-fronted section overlooking the Place Centrale fills up with ski-booted après seekers. Various live bands strum out old favourites to the receptive and enthusiastic audience, who sing along at full volume. The rear part of the bar is more subdued - one half (known as Cigarillos) is a cosy corner with a few enveloping leather chairs and sofas, which are rarely free. In the other half the less comfortable wooden chairs and tables are positioned towards the small television where you can watch UK and European football matches. For the 6 Nations rugby and the Grand National, a bigger screen is set up. You can also enjoy a drink on the terrace beside the hotel entrance.

hotel vanessa

map - town c/d2
t 027 775 2800
open late
food only in hotel restaurant
tv ✗

Words cannot adequately describe this quirky hotel bar. The pure kitsch décor pays homage to the 1980s, whilst an enthusiastic pianist crones to his favourite back catalogue of love songs and ABBA medleys. The Sicilian barman, François, mixes a decent drink and can do "amazing things with fruit" - just don't be surprised if he contributes to the croning.

king's bar

map - town b2
t 027 775 2037
open 7pm - 1:30pm
food ✗
tv ✗

On entering King's, you'll feel you've stumbled across a hidden gem. In reality, it is a well known venue, but it never gets over-busy - the high prices making it somewhere best kept for special or extravagant occasions. The small room has the refined air and appearance of a chic members-only club, but the atmosphere is always laid-back. The cocktail list is satisfying long, with some mouth-wateringly unusual creations, like a grape martini or a passion fruit caiparinhia. And if you're planning to be there for a while, re-mortgage your house first.

le fer à cheval

map - town e3
t 027 771 2669
open 9:30am-11:30pm
food all day
tv ×

A mainstay of the après scene, most visitors make it to the Furry at some point during their stay. A lively venue from mid-afternoon, you need to get ahead of the hordes to be guaranteed one of the prime tables on the terrace - or any of the occasional free pizza. If you are planning a long stay a table inside is better, as the terrace soon falls into the shade. Even then, unless you stay for dinner, après ends when the restaurant starts its service at 7pm. Any ski instructor stalkers should start here - the Furry is a favourite watering-hole of many a Jean-Noël and Edouard you might have admired on the slopes.

murphy's bar

map - town d3
t 027 771 6272
open 2pm - 2am
food ×
tv ×

Murphy's Bar on the ground floor of Hotel Garbo suffers from something of an identity crisis. It aims for sophistication with a tempting cocktail menu, but the inside resembles an empty warehouse. The void doesn't matter when the bar is busy, but when quiet it can feel cavernous and empty. Cocktail orders can be greeted with derision or confusion, so get to know your bar staff before parting with CHF15 for a quickly-drunk mojito. Après here can be subdued, except on sunny days when people gravitate to the palm-tree-decked terrace on the roof of the bar, which is open from 2pm until sunset. The inside bar is more of a late evening venue, and fills up from 10pm onwards. Lively theme nights are a regular event here - mardi gras especially should not be missed.

95

nelson pub

map - town c2
t 027 771 3151
open 11am-1:30pm
food ×
tv ✓

For the home-sick few, the Nelson is the best medicine in Verbier. Truly resembling a traditional English pub, inside is all dark wood furniture, chintzy wallpaper and a smoky atmosphere. The picture is completed by a darts board and a pool table. Situated just off the Place Centrale, gamblers will be keen to know that it also houses Verbier's only betting shop.

pub mont fort

map - town e4
t 027 771 4898
open 3pm-1:30am
food ✓ (4pm-10pm)
tv for special events

Something of a Marmite bar, you'll either love it or hate it here. Busy, young and in need of a face-lift, Le Pub is inexplicably popular. When the sun shines, the large terrace fills with seasonnaires making the most of Verbier's only happy hour (4pm-5pm). After 5pm, drinks double in price - so buy your round before then or make the most of one of the regular drinks promotions. Better still, befriend a seasonnaire, as they get discounted drinks all night, which is presumably why an above average quota of chalet girls and boys, reps and *plongeurs* drink here. After the mid-evening lull, the two floors of this large pub fill up again - downstairs tends to be more chilled out, although it does host the 'Shooters Bar'. Le Pub holds regular theme nights, but don't expect to get in if you're 'in theme'. If you want to check your email, there is an internet terminal in a small alcove off the main bar.

96

snapshot

what to drink...

France, Spain, and New Zealand - all countries you associate with fine **wine**. But Switzerland? Not somewhere that immediately springs to mind, but either the altitude or the holiday-spirit make the local Valais wine quite drinkable. Fendant is a light, crisp, dry white whilst Dôle is a fruity red, a blend of Pinot Noir and Gamay grapes. Or the Dôle Blanche is an enjoyable rosé. If you want something warm there is always vin chaud - a combination of hot red wine brewed with spices.

Beer also doesn't seem very Swiss, but they must have taken tips from their neighbours, as the national ales such as Cardinal aren't bad. You can buy better known lagers for slightly more CHF. For something different, try the cloudy German weissbier, or a *panaché* (lager shandy) for refreshment - it doesn't carry the stigma it does in the UK.

For those with steel-lined stomachs or a masochistic appetite, the local fire-water is **Willamine** (a pear-based schnapps). Some restaurants offer a shot of this or something equally evil on the house, to round off your meal - perhaps the generous nature of the Swiss... or simply the restaurant trying to get rid of you?

nightclubs

All of the bars are closed by 1:30am, but the nightclubs are open to 4am to entertain those not so keen to catch the first lift. Nightclubs in ski resorts are often an interesting phenomen, and often seem to be the place where bad records go when they retire. Fortunately Verbier's clubs understand slightly better what their clientele want to dance to and play a little less unrecognisable German techno than you might hear else where.

useful information

boys v girls - at weekends and on busier evenings, the more girls in your group, the quicker you will get in, just like any club in the world.

dress code - none of the clubs have a dress policy, so there's no need to dig out the glad rags - you'll get in even in jeans and outdoor boots.

prices

No surprises - drinks are expensive. Spirits can be bought by the bottle and mixers are then provided free - if you are part of a group - or will go back most nights - this works out as fairly good value. If you don't finish your bottle in one sitting, the bar will hold it for you until you finish it, even if it takes all season. Cover charges vary from place to place - only the Farm doesn't have one - and also what time you arrive. Cloakrooms also levy a minimal fee.

the farm

map - town b1
t 027 771 6121
open 11pm-4am (closed Sundays)
entrance free

Verbier's most infamous nightclub is best for star-gazers and celebrity spotters - Fergie was a regular when she worked in Verbier as a chalet girl. Now, the Farm still attracts an affluent crowd, happy to spend CHF200 on a bottle of spirits, so it's a great place to people-watch. Make sure you get there before 11:30pm on Fridays and Saturdays just to get in - and even if you reserve a table, you shouldn't expect more than one by the door if you're a Farm virgin. The door policy is a bit Jekyll and Hyde - you're greeted like a long lost friend on the quieter week nights, and given something of the cold shoulder at weekends. But this cool treatment doesn't deter the ever-eager crowds jostling for position at the door - when standing in line, it helps to look lovely and loaded and that you intend to part with your cash.

marshal's

map - town c3
t 027 771 6626
open 11pm-4am (closed Mondays and Tuesdays)
entrance free until 12am, then CHF10

A much younger crowd dances at Marshal's. The latest street clothes are obligatory and it helps if you know

97

nightclubs

your ollies from your nollies. Shots of lurid coloured drinks are often given out free at the entrance to entice you in. Once inside, you can continue downing shots (though you'll have to pay for them), treat yourself to a bottle of spirits or even eat a few snacks to maintain your stamina. The club is quite small, so even when it isn't completely full, it can still seem busy. It's also home to the even smaller Aristo Bar - a tiny room at the far end of the club.

98

taratata

map - town c3
t 027 771 4535/079 456 2502
open 11:30pm-4am
entrance free until 1:30am, then CHF20

Underneath the Hotel Bristol and known more commonly as Tara's, the clientele is younger and hipper than at the Farm and the attitude is more about having fun than being the most beautiful. The music seems to be selected by its danceability rating, which helps keep the dance-floor well populated. As with the Farm, the door policy can be unfriendly when they don't need your business, but welcoming when they do. Tara's has a proactive approach to upping its girl ratio, often letting girls in for free after 1:30am or on certain nights of the week.

snapshot

high days and holidays
Christmas starts early - the Swiss welcome the arrival of St. Nicholas on 6th December and celebrations reach their peak on Christmas Eve when families and friends exchange presents. If you holiday over Christmas, you won't find a turkey dinner on offer in the restaurants - although if you are stay in a chalet run by a tour operator, they will normally provide the full works.

On **new year's eve** most residents and visitors gather in the Place Centrale to celebrate with fireworks, champagne and music. The bars and clubs then open until the early morning and the survivors meet for breakfast in Offshore. All the clubs and some bars are ticketed - expect to pay CHF50 to CHF100 just to get in. Many of the restaurants serve a special dinner - as most get booked up days before, don't expect to find a table without a reservation.

The week of **mardi gras** is also a cause for celebration. On Shrove Tuesday, it is *de rigueur* to wear fancy dress if you're going out. The Swiss really go to town with their costumes - the more outrageous the better - and many of the pubs and bars will think twice about letting you in unless you've at least made a token effort to join in.

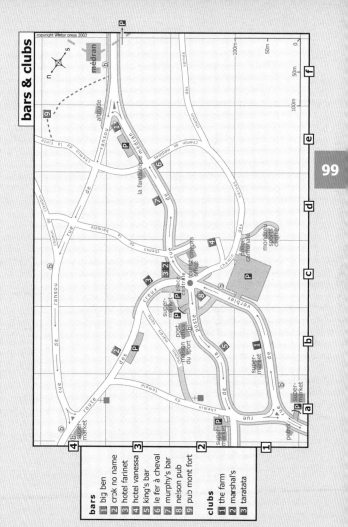

bars & clubs

copyright winter press 2003

99

bars

1. big ben
2. crok no name
3. hotel farinet
4. hotel vanessa
5. king's bar
6. le fer à cheval
7. murphy's bar
8. nelson pub
9. pub mont fort

clubs

1. the farm
2. marshal's
3. taratata

hotels

One word - expensive. And it's
debatable whether you get value for
money. As in England, Swiss hotels
are graded from 1* to 5* - but here
the similarity stops. Stars are
awarded for factors such as room size
and whether the hotel has a
restaurant offering an evening
meal. The facilities one 4* hotel
offers can be very different from
another, depending upon how it
earned its stars. The result is that on
appearances alone it is difficult to
work out exactly what you'll get. Price
is generally the best guide.

100

useful information

access - none of Verbier's hotels are
ski in/ski out, some are better placed
for the lift stations and some for the
bars and restaurants. Comments note
each hotel's location to the village and
Médran or Savoleyres, or whether they
offer a free shuttle service.

bookings - you can contact the hotel
directly, or book through a tour
operator or travel agent. The tourist
office offers week packages (Saturday
to Saturday) during low and mid
season for some of the hotels - book
by phone or through the tourist office
website.

Most of the hotels will only consider a
booking for less than a week if it is
made within 2 weeks of the date you
want to arrive. As a general rule

---

snapshot

for...
• a last minute deal - bristol garni
• families - vanessa
• good food - montpelier
• liveliness - farinet
• location, location - rosalp
• peace & quiet - les 4 vallées
• luxury - chalet d'adrien
• weekend availability - les rois mages

though, booking policies are most
flexible during low season.

equipment rental - many hotels
have a deal with a specific rental shop
- they will advise you of this when you
check in. The rental shop mentioned in
each review is the nearest one to that
hotel, intended to help you to avoid
spending time lugging your rental skis
halfway across town.

facilities - unless otherwise stated,
all bedrooms are en-suite, with a
shower or bath. At a *Garni*, only bed
and breakfast is available. All hotels
have a lift, and parking in either a
private car park or the hotel garage.

prices

In this guide hotels are divided into
three price categories - what you can
expect to pay for a double room per
night in high season, including tax but
not service.
luxury above CHF400
mid-range CHF200-400
budget below CHF200

verbier lodge ***

map - valley d4
t 027 771 6666
f 027 771 6656
e info@verbierlodge.ch
i verbierlodge.ch
rooms 13
board b&b
shuttle ✓
ski hire fellay sports II (town f4)

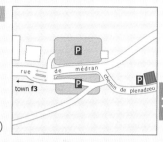

Opened in 2003, the Lodge is a sport hotel aimed at serious skiers. Tucked away in the forest to the east of the village, it is only a 5 minute walk from Médran. You can reserve accommodation only or opt for one of the board & ski packages, which include ski instruction.

Rooms are named after different ski resorts - so let them know your favourite if you have one... although for an unimpaired view, a room on the second floor or higher is best. There are three suites, and some rooms have balconies. Apart from one suite, all rooms only have showers, so those who need a bath-tub to ease away their aches and pains will be disappointed. That said, the sauna, hammam and outdoor hot-tub help and are more luxurious than the 3* rating suggests. There is also a small gym for those wanting to get in some last minute fitness training.

The Lodge makes a slightly optimistic bid to promote its bar for après-ski - you can ski to it by following the signs on the blue piste down to Médran - but residents may be keen for it to remain a secret, as it is a pleasant spot for a drink, and is far from the madding crowd in the centre of the village.

« luxury »

chalet d'adrien*****

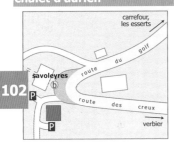

102

map - valley b5
t 027 771 6200
f 027 771 6224
e info@chalet-adrien.com
i chalet-adrien.com
rooms 19 rooms and 6 suites
board b&b/½
shuttle ✓
ski hire evasion sports (valley b5)

Verbier's only 5* hotel, and with a price tag to match. A Relais & Chateaux, it is small and luxurious, and is perched above the village next to Savoleyres - which some find inconvenient for the shops and restaurants. But you need not worry about going hungry - the hotel has two restaurants, L'Astrance for haute cuisine and Le Grenier for less extravagant dining, and on sunny days lunch is served on a expansive terrace with its hard-to-beat view up the valley. Rooms are individually and tastefully furnished and most face south and the hotel has an appealing sauna, hot tub and hammam.

king's parc****

map - town b1
t 027 775 2010
f 027 775 2034
e info@kingsverbier.ch
i kingsverbier.ch
rooms 26
board b&b/½
shuttle ✓
ski hire médran sports (town b1)

Behind the Hotel Rhodania, the King's Parc is in the heart of the village, but it is a 20 minute uphill walk to Médran if you don't take the free shuttle. All rooms are spacious suites and each has a living area in addition to the bedroom. On a cold and snowy day, it can be hard to get beyond the inviting lobby and lounge, because of its log fire, well-stocked bar, comfortable leather chairs, and in the afternoon its tempting cake trolley. The hotel houses an excellent, highly rated restaurant - also called King's - which offers a menu of "modern food with pacific-rim influences". Enough said.

montpelier****

map - valley b4
t 027 771 6131
f 027 771 4689
e hotel-montpelier@verbier.ch
i hotelmontpelier.ch
rooms 46
board b&b/½
shuttle ✓
ski hire jet (town a1)

The Montpelier's only drawback is its location - it's a 30 minute walk to the Médran or Savoleyres lift stations and 20 minutes to the centre - but the excellent facilities mean you only need to leave to go skiing. The hotel has a spa with a small indoor pool where you can swim whilst admiring the view, large bedrooms decorated in stencilled wood, and one of the finest restaurants in Verbier, which serves excellent haute cuisine food. The best room is the magnificent penthouse, which has its own log fire. But if that's beyond your budget, you can warm yourself by the one in the lounge. Service throughout is polite and unobtrusive.

rosalp****

map - town e3
t 027 771 6323
f 027 771 1059
e rosalp@verbier.ch
i rosalp.ch
rooms 19 and 4 suites
board b&b/½
shuttle ✓
ski hire the ski center (town e3)

Another Relais & Chateaux, the Rosalp is Verbier's best known 4* hotel. Opened in the 1940s by the Pierroz family, it is now famous for Roland Pierroz, its Michelin starred chef and owner. Centrally located in the heart of the shops, restaurants and bars, it is less than a 5 minute walk from Médran. Of all the 4* hotels, the Rosalp takes itself the most seriously and the atmosphere is more reserved and more formal than elsewhere. Some bedrooms would benefit from being a little bigger but the rest of the facilities are top-class - guests with weary muscles from a tough day on the slopes will enjoy the leisure facilities and the attentions of the in-house masseur.

« mid-range »

les 4 vallées garni****

map - town e3
t 027 775 3344
f 027 775 3345
e les4vallees@verbier.ch
i les4vallees.com
rooms 20
board b&b
shuttle ✓
ski hire the ski center (town e3)

A very good value choice, the 4 Vallées is a small, friendly, family-run hotel. Only breakfast is served, but as it's located on Rue de Médran, there are plenty of restaurants nearby. The en-suite rooms are reminiscent of the 1970s, with avocado bathrooms and orange and brown furnishings, but the cleanliness and warmth more than

103

compensate. Most rooms face south and have stunning views over the valley. Nothing is too much trouble - your ski boots are dried overnight, and the cosy bar will stay open as long as you need it to. Sadly for animal lovers, pets are not allowed.

les rois mages****

map - valley b/c5
t 027 771 6364
f 027 771 3319
e info@skiverbier.com
i skiverbier.co.uk
rooms 15
board b&b
shuttle ✓
ski hire fellay sports I (town c3)

The 'Wise Kings' is a curiosity in Verbier, being the only hotel run by a ski company (Ski Verbier). Having only 15 bedrooms, it feels more like a chalet than a hotel, which in some ways is reflected by the service you receive. In the hotel itself, two managers look after your needs whilst the other aspects of your holiday - such as lift passes and lessons - are organised by the Ski Verbier reps. Located a 2 minute walk from the distinctive Catholic church, the Rois Mages welcomes weekend stayers and has a flexible booking policy should you wish to stay for less a week. Children are welcome - during school holidays special evening meals and babysitting services are available on request, and there is a playroom for children.

vanessa****

map - town c/d2
t 027 775 2800
f 027 775 2828
e vanessa@verbier.ch
rooms 55
board b&b/$^1/_2$
shuttle ✓
ski hire dany sports (town c/d2)

One of Verbier's larger hotels, the Vanessa is ideal for families, or groups of friends who want to stay in a hotel - some of its duplexes can sleep up to six in one apartment. Despite needing a decorative overhaul, the family-like atmosphere is what brings people back - service is quirky but friendly and you'll soon feel more like a good friend than a guest. Located just off the Place Centrale and only a 10 minute walk from Médran, most of Verbier's attractions are within easy reach. If you self-drive, you can park for a small daily fee in the hotel garage.

bristol garni***

map - town c3
t 027 771 6577
f 027 771 5150

e hotel.bristol@verbier.ch
i bristol-verbier.ch
rooms 31
board b&b
shuttle ×
ski hire fellay sports I (town c3)

An ideal hotel for those wanting to be close to the action without paying over the odds. The Bristol is located above the Pharmacie de Verbier on Route des Creux, just up from the Place Centrale. Everything you need is on the doorstep - Borsalino or Le Caveau for eating, the Farinet for drinking and Tara's (underneath the hotel) for dancing. The hotel was renovated in 1999 and though the rooms are sparsely furnished they are clean and of an ample size. In the reception there is a free internet connection and a surprising amount of information about Sweden.

farinet***

map - town c3
t 027 771 6626
f 027 771 3855
e farinet@axiom.ch
i hotelfarinet.ch
rooms 21
board b&b/½
shuttle ×
ski hire xtreme sports (town c2)

At the heart of the village above the Place Centrale, the Farinet is better known for après-ski. The rooms are comfortable, although some have been more recently renovated than others. The hotel is reasonably well sound-proofed, but if you are a light

sleeper or know you'll want an afternoon nap, ask to be on a higher floor, so you're not disturbed by noise from the bar. The atmosphere in the hotel is youthful - perhaps created by the staff, most of whom are in their 20s or 30s. Most speak English as a first language, so you will alway so understood. The restaurant on the ground floor - where you take breakfast - is known as Marco's, and serves decent classic Italian food in the evenings.

105

mazot***

map - town d1/2
t 027 775 3550
f 027 775 3555
e mazot@verbier.ch
i hotelmazot.ch
rooms 25
board b&b/½
shuttle ×
ski hire dany sports (town c/d2)

Mazot means 'Swiss Home', and accordingly you will feel welcome as soon as you arrive. A long corridor of a hotel, there are fewer bedrooms than the building size suggests, so you have plenty of space. The staff are extremely friendly and helpful and speak good English. The hotel is a 2 minute walk from the Place Centrale, 10 minutes from Médran, and the Mondzeu swimming pool is just across the road. You can park for free outside the hotel, or in its garage for a small daily fee. Other facilities include a sauna, a solarium and free internet connection in the hotel lobby.

« budget »

map - town d3
t 027 771 6272
f 027 771 6271
e hotelgarbo@verbier.ch
i hotelgarbo.com
    rooms 25
    board b&b/¹/₂
    shuttle ×
    ski hire ski service (town d3)

106

None of Verbier's hotels are truly 'budget' - some are cheaper than others, but few are good value. Garbo's wins inclusion because of its location - 5 minutes from Médran and in the middle of the après-ski fun (including the hotel's own bar), meaning you will rarely be alone - and because it is less frequently used by tour operators. The bedrooms are small and contain the bare essentials - and have little space for much else. A good continental breakfast is served in what becomes Garbo's restaurant in the evening.

map - valley b4/5
t 027 771 6602
f 027 771 6603
e sleep@thebunker.ch
i thebunker.ch
rooms 3 dormitories
board ¹/₂
shuttle ✓
ski hire jet (town a1)

Truly a budget offering, the Bunker is a hostel rather than a hotel. Located in the *Centre Sportif*, accommodation is available in one of two very different buildings. The Bunker itself is an old nuclear shelter, with five entirely underground dormitories - though you'll never see the sun at least you know you'll be safe in the event of an atomic attack. For the princely sum of CHF45 you get a bed (for which you need to bring your own sheets) free entrance to the swimming pool and ice rink, breakfast, a 3-course evening meal, and digital TV and video. Accommodation in dormitories or double rooms is also available in the nearby Summer House. Slightly more expensive than the Bunker, perhaps because of the need to clean and maintain windows, priority is given to one week rentals.

hotels

copyright winter press 2003

107

hotels

1. king's parc
2. rosalp
3. 4 vallées garni
4. vanessa
5. tristol garni
6. farinet
7. mazot
8. garbo

activities

When the lifts are closed because of too little - or more frustratingly - too much snow, or your muscles just can't take any more, the resort and surrounding area offer a few attractions to keep you occupied. For all contact details see the **directory**.

108

sports

sports centres & swimming - the Verbier *Centre Sportif* (**valley b4/5**) is a large complex just off Rue de Centre Sportif and is unmissable because of its distinctive roof made of hexagonal-shaped panels. The facilities are extensive - a 12mx25m indoor heated pool, a 30mx60m indoor ice-rink, tennis and squash courts, a sauna, Turkish bath and solarium suite, a curling rink and an indoor climbing wall. Open 10am-9pm every day, you can pay as you go - how much you pay depends upon what you want to do - or buy a 7 day holiday pass. Lessons in swimming and climbing are possible during the winter months.

You can also swim at the Mondzeu swimming pool (**town d1**) - smaller than the Centre Sportif and generally quieter. More centrally located it is only a 2 minute walk from the Place Centrale. Facilities include an indoor heated pool (10x20m) and a sauna and a fitness centre. It is open every day (except Wednesday) 10am-12pm

and 3pm-8pm. You can pay as you go or buy a book of tickets at a reduced price, good for three visits.

ice climbing - with over twenty ice cascades in the Val de Bagnes area during the winter months, ice climbing is a popular sport. The uninitiated first climb an artifical pyramid before progressing to the frozen waterfalls. Instruction can be booked through any of the ski schools or guiding companies.

indoor golf - you can keep your swing going whilst you are away - the indoor golf centre on Rue de Ransou (**town d4**) has a driving range, a simulator, a swing analysis and a putting green.

parapenting - you can't fail to notice the colourful parachutes circling overhead on a sunny day. You can join them for an hour's tandem flight or even a course. Either option can be booked with the parapenting schools, Centre de Parapente (also bookable through the Maison du Sport), L'Envol and Max Biplace (also bookable through La Fantastique). On average, a hour's flight costs CHF170.

walking - a popular pastime, particularly amongst the locals, even in the winter. For information on lift pass discounts see **getting started** and see **non-skiers** for information on the groomed pathways.

culture

cinema - Verbier's small, theatre-like cinema (**town c2**) shows mainstream English and American blockbusters and some French films. Each film is shown twice a day for two days, normally at 6pm or 6:30pm and again at 8:30pm or 9pm, along with a childrens matinee and an extra screening during bad weather or the school holidays. See the fortnightly leaflet for details of the screenings. Entrance is CHF15-22.

museums & galleries - if you're interested in alpine history, the museum at Le Hameau (**valley c5**) displays relics of the history of and civilisation in the Alps. Le Hameau also houses the biggest conference centre in the village and the world's largest sundial. Just beyond the nursery slope at Les Esserts, it is open Tuesday to Friday 10am-12pm and 1:30pm-6pm. For art-lovers, the Galerie d'Art La Foret at Le Hameau opens Mondays 10am-12pm, Thursday to Saturday 10am-12pm and 4pm-7pm.

further afield

If the sometimes claustraphobic atmosphere of the resort gets too much Lavey les Bains and Martigny are both within easy reach of Verbier and are worth a visit.

lavey les bains - unsurprisingly for an area known for its spring water, thermal spas are in abundance and the baths at Lavey (just off the A9) are the best. Originally built to treat patients suffering from a range of ailments, now most people make a trip to the baths just to relax. Set underneath an imposing face of rock, the complex has a huge outdoor pool with water jets and whirlpools, all at comfortably warm temperatures, ranging from 30°C to 36°C. Open daily 9am-9pm, you can also enjoy the indoor pool, hammams and saunas.

109

martigny - the oldest town in the canton, Martigny sits on the banks of the Rhône river. Some of the buildings date back to Roman times, including the striking Bâtiaz Castle, which you can see as you approach the town on the motorway from Geneva. Now, it is a pleasant market town, with tree-lined streets and a mixture of high-street shops and quirky boutiques. Away from the shopping the big attractions include the Roman ampitheatre and the Fondation Pierre Gianadda, which has regular art exhibitions and musical concerts.

Towards the end of the season, the Combats des Reines (cow fights) are held in Martigny and throughout Valais. Historically held so the local cows could battle out who got to lead the herd up the hill to the summer pasture, now the emphasis is more on breeding the 'queen' of the herd and on having a good time.

children

Compared to the 3 Vallées, the facilities for children are more limited. Few of the tour operators offer the kids clubs and childcare available elsewhere and the resort itself is not amazingly equipped, perhaps because Verbier is not strongly promoted as a destination for families. Below is a summary of the childcare and ski school options and other activities offered.

tour operators

Many operators offer discounted or free child places in their chalets and will provide a special meal for children in the evenings. Some also include free ski and boot hire, lift passes or ski lessons for childen in their packages. However, almost none of them - except **simply ski** - offer their own childcare programme and you will have to rely on the resort's kindergarten and crèche facilities. If you book the whole of one of Simply Ski's chalets, they will provide a private nanny service - for children aged 6 months to 8 years, up to a maximum of three children. Whichever operator you book with, make sure to request a cot or high-chair if you need one.

childcare

babysitters - for short-term childcare, the tourist office keeps a list of registered babysitters - expect to pay CHF15-25 per hour. Another option is one of the hundreds of English-speaking seasonnaires who are happy to earn a few extra CHF.

kindergarten/crèche - **les schtroumpfs** (**town a2**) (**t** 027 771 6585) is a non-skiing day centre based in Chalet Lesberty run by Brigitte Tisseres. The crèche will take children aged between 3 months to 4 years and all staff are qualified carers. The centre is open Monday to Saturday 8:30am-5:30pm and 9:30am-5:30pm on Sundays. You can leave your child for a full day - lunch is provided - or a half-day (8:30am-11:30am or 1:30pm-5:30pm). Book ahead as the crèche can only accept a limited number of children and remember your child's medical vaccination certificates.

ski school

maison du sport, **la fantastique** and **altitude** - see **ski schools** - run group lessons from Monday to Saturday for children aged from 3 to 12 years. Children must wear a helmet to join a group lesson. Make sure it fits well - childrens' heads don't grow as quickly as their body, so they should be able to use it for a couple of years. You can buy an animal cover to make it more appealing.

The cost of these lessons does not include a lift pass. As the majority of them take place on the main pistes, all children whatever their age must have one - see **lift passes**.

Group lessons may not be the ideal way for all children to learn how to ski or board, but there are a couple of other options.

maison du sport kids club

map valley b5
t 027 775 3363
open monday to saturday, 8:30am-5pm
age 3-6 years

Learning to ski is the main activity at the Kids Club. Based at Les Moulins in a specially-designed garden it is a safer and less threatening place to learn than the main pistes, with a gentle ski slope, escalator and baby-lift. You can leave your child for a full or half-day (8:30am-11:15am or 1:30pm-5pm) and lunch is available.

les elfes

map valley b5
t 027 775 3590
f 027 775 3599
e leselfes@verbier.ch
i leselfes.com
open all year
age 8-22 years

Les Elfes is an international children's camp. Children stay in 1 of 2 specially designed chalets - linked by a tunnel. During the day children learn to ski or board with trained instructors - many of whom are English. After skiing and in the evening other activities - such as squash, swimming and sledging - are organised. Language classes In English, German or French are an optional extra.

other activities

on the snow - Maison du Sport run night-skiing once or twice a week at Les Esserts and a torchlit descent from Les Ruinettes every Wednesday evening aimed at children. A small supper is served first at Les Ruinettes, and then at about 6pm the children ski down accompanied by Maison du Sport instructors.

111

off the snow - the cinema shows a childrens film at 5pm. When the weather is bad enough to close most of the lifts, an extra screening is shown, normally at 3pm or 3:30pm.

After the day's skiing, *Le Sentier Suspendu* (the Suspended Walkway) is a fun activity for children and adults alike. A series of ropes, walkways and bridges hang from trees in the forest just past Médran. A harness and a helmet are provided, and you are accompanied by a guide. There is also a 4-faced climbing tower. Book through the Maison du Sport. Children must be taller than 120cm.

eating & drinking

Most of Verbier's restaurants and cafés welcome children - the friendliest are **borsalino**, **chez martin** and **offshore** (see **food & drink**) - and some offer a childrens menu. Children are generally allowed into the bars and pubs and it is up to you whether they drink - generally nobody bats an eyelid if a child or teenager drinks wine with their parents.

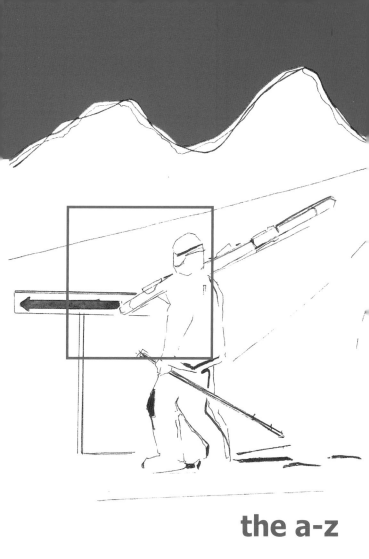

the a-z

directory

listings

All 027, 024 and 022 numbers need the Swiss international prefix (0041) if dialled from the UK.

Where applicable, references are given to the town map.

accidents

If you have an accident on the slopes, you will be taken to the nearest doctor unless you specify a particular one. To confirm you can pay for treatment carry a credit card and your insurance details. At some point, contact your insurance company to check whether they want to arrange your transport home. And ask your doctor for a medical certificate confirming you are fit to travel.

If you see an accident on the slopes, tell the nearest rescue centre, normally at the top or bottom of lifts.

activities

cinema (**c2**) **t** 027 771 2435

ice climbing - see under **guides**

indoor golf (**d4**) **t** 027 771 6108

lavey les bains t 024 486 1555
i lavey-les-bains.ch

museum & galleries

le hameau t 027 771 7560
i lehameau.ch
galerie la foret t 027 771 8700

parapenting

centre parapente t 027 771 6818,
i flyverbier.ch
ecole l'envol t 079 679 9452
max biplace t 027 771 55 55/079 219 36 55

sports centres & swimming

centre sportif t 027 771 6601,
i verbier-sports.ch
mondzeu (**d1**) **t** 027 771 4158

snow activities

heliskiing
air glaciers t 027 329 1415
i air-glaciers.ch
& see **ski schools** in **getting started**

snowshoeing
see **ski schools** in **getting started**

apartments & private chalets

interhome t 0208 891 1294
i interhome.co.uk
powderwhite i powderwhite.co.uk
verbier chalet t 027 771 9630
i verbierchalet.com

army

100 or so UK squaddies and officers stay for 6 weeks from early December for ski training and racing. They can make their presence felt around the resort, but you soon get to know - and avoid - the venues they favour.

banks & ATMs

banque cantonale du valais (**c2**) and **UBS** (**c2**) on the Place Centrale,

directory

banque edouard constant (**b2**) on Rue de la Poste and **credit suisse** (**b1**) on Rue de Verbier open Monday to Friday 9am-12pm and 3pm-6pm. All have 24 hour ATMs, which often run out of money at weekends.

car hire
geneva airport
ALAMO t 022 717 8430
i alamo.com
AVIS t 022 929 0330 **i** avis.com
easycar t 0906 333 3333
i easycar.com
europcar t 022 798 1110
i europcar.com
hertz t 0870 844 8844 **i** hertz.com

verbier
AVIS t 027 771 3666
hertz t/f 027 771 4553/6362

church services
The Catholic church (**a3**) holds services in French at 6pm on Saturdays and 11:30am and 6pm on Sundays. A Protestant service in English is held in the Swiss Reformed church (**a2**) at 6pm on Sundays. At 2:30pm on Wednesdays in good weather a *priere du skieur* is held in La Chaux.

customs
UK visitors over 17 can take 200 cigarettes, 50 cigars or 250g of pipe tobacco, 1 litre of alcohol over 15% proof, 2 litres of alcohol below 15% proof and gifts up to the value of CHF100 out of Switzerland.

doctor
All of the medical centres are open Monday to Friday 8:30am-12pm and 2pm-6pm and Saturday mornings - **cabinet medical des arcades** (**a1**) (**t** 027 771 7020/for emergencies 079 447 2572) underneath Migros, **cabinet medical square poste** (**b2**) (**t** 027 771 7001) off Rue de la Poste and **polyclinique verbier** (**c3**) (**t** 027 771 6677) on Route des Creux. The nearest **hospital** is in **martigny** (**t** 027 603 9000).

The medical centres operate an on-call rota (which is displayed in the tourist office) at night, on Sundays and bank holidays.

driving
general - carry a valid driver's licence, proof of ownership, your insurance certificate and an emergency triangle.

speed limits - in villages and suburbs the speed limit is 50km/h (unless indicated). The limit is 80km/h on all other roads and 120km/h on motorways.

signs & rules - motorway signs are green and you need a *vignette* (a windscreen sticker) to travel on them - buy one at the border. They last for the year in which bought and cost CHF40. You must wear a seatbelt in the front and back of a car. Children under 12 must sit in the back and babies and young children must be

directory

placed in special baby/young child seats. Important rules for driving in the mountains are that ascending vehicles have priority and postal buses and pedestrians always have right of way. A handbook on road signs and regulations is available in English from the cantonale police.

electricity
220 volts/50hz ac. Appliances use a two-pin plug - you can buy adaptors at Geneva airport or in Verbier at **swisscom** on Rue de la Poste.

emergency numbers
police t 117
ambulance t 144
fire brigade t 118
24/7 road assistance t 140
bloodwagon t 027 775 2511
air ambulance t 1414
air glaciers t 1415
euro emergency t 112
on-call dentist t 079 606 0550
on-call pharmacy t 0900 558 143

From a phone box, emergency calls are not always free so you may need some change to make the call.

guides
bureau des guides t 027 775 3364
ski club of gb rep t 079 580 3639
& see **ski schools** in **getting started**

independent
alpine guides t 079 446 2289
i swissguides.com
mountain experience t 01663 750

160, **i** mountain experience.co.uk
olivier roduit t 079 206 9790/027 771 5317, **i** mountain-guide.ch

health
UK visitors don't need any vaccinations to enter Switzerland. There isn't a national health service, so you pay for treatment when you receive it.

insurance
Personal insurance covering wintersports and the cost of any ambulances, helicopter rescue and emergency repatriation is essential as all these services are expensive. Insurance policies differ greatly - some exclude off-piste skiing or cover it only if you go with a guide, so check the terms and conditions carefully. Also ensure that après-ski activities, such as tobogganing, are covered. If you do not have any cover before you arrive in Verbier you can buy an Air Glaciers card for CHF30 from any of TéléVerbier's offices.

internet/email
harold's hamburgers (**c2**) has five iMacs for word processing or internet access. Open 10am-1:30am, non-members pay CHF1 to log-in and then 30 cents a minute, and members pay 50 cents to log-in (after an initial payment of CHF30) and then 20 cents a minute.

Elsewhere, the **pub mont fort** (**e4**) has a metered terminal in a small

directory

alcove off the main pub, whilst the **verbier beach** restaurant in the Centre Sportif has two terminals.

Most phone boxes also have an internet/email facility.

language
Verbier is in French-speaking Switzerland, though information is also displayed in Swiss-German and Italian. English is widely spoken.

laundry & dry cleaning
les arcades (**a1**) by Migros, **charmarel** (**c3**) on Rue de Médran and **mirella** (**b3**) on Route des Creux.

left luggage
You can leave your luggage at the **post office** (**b2**) on Rue de la Poste.

library (**b1**)
Open (**t** 027 771 1101) 4pm-6pm on Wednesdays and Fridays and 10am-12pm on Saturdays, 20% of the books are in English. All visitors can obtain temporary membership.

lift pass office
téléverbier (**f4**) (**t/f** 027 775 2511/2599, **i** televerbier.ch) issues lift passes at Médran and Savoleyres.

maps
The tourist office has A4-sized maps of the village. OS maps (1:50000 or 1:25000) of the surrounding area are available from the **naville** (**c2**) on the Place Centrale.

massage
massage and therapy centre martine michellod (**b2**) (by appointment) **t** 027 771 7180, **ambrosia** (**d4**) **t** 079 332 4430/027 771 2177, **artemis** (**b3**) **t** 027 771 2158, **océane** (**b2**) **t** 027 771 6170, **à fleur de peau t** 079 611 2826.

money
The currency is the Swiss Franc (SFr/CHF) - CHF1 is 100 centimes. Notes come in CHF10, 20, 50, 100, 200, 1,000 and coins in CHF1, 2, 5 and cents 5, 10, 20, 50. In 2003 the average exchange rate for UK£1 was CHF2.2. Some places accept Euros.

You can exchange money in all the banks in Verbier during the week and also at the airport and train stations. You can change money at the tourist office, TéléVerbier or the 'Bazar' at the Vallée Blanche on Rue de Médran at weekends. You can change CHF notes for CHF coins at the change machine at Médran.

newspapers
English newspapers (and others) - often for the same day - are available from the **naville** (**c2**) on the Place Centrale and the small kiosk next to the post office. Expect to pay three times what you would pay in the UK.

parking
Parking along the roads is only allowed where indicated and the police will give you a ticket if you are

directory

illegally parked.

pay & display long term
Médran 8am-4pm (270 spaces)
Place Centrale 8am-8pm (127 spaces)
Savoleyres lift station (70 spaces)
free long term
Centre Sportif (500 places)
Carrefour (15 places)
Les Esserts (60 places)
pay & display short term
Route des Creux (18 places)
free short term
underneath Migros, underneath
Primo, next to Coop and by the
Rosalp hotel on Rue de Médran.

passport photos
There are two booths at Médran (**f4**).

passports & visas
UK citizens don't need a visa but your
passport should have at least 6
months until expiry. UK visitors can
stay for 3 months (although passports
are rarely stamped) - and you need a
work permit for a longer stay (see
under **seasonnaires**). All Swiss
citizens must carry personal ID, so it's
a good idea to carry your passport
with you.

petrol
Petrol stations are rarely open at
night, but most have automatic
distributors, which accept credit cards
or cash. Instructions are rarely in
English so they can be confusing to
use. Verbier has two petrol stations -
one on Rue de Verbier (**a1**) and one
on Rue de Centre Sportif.

pharmacies
pharmacie internationale (**c2**) (**t**
027 771 6622) on Rue de Médran and
pharmacie de verbier (**c3**) (**t** 027
771 2330) on Route des Creux open
Monday to Saturday 8:30am-12:30pm
and 2:30pm-7pm and Sundays 10am-
12:30pm and 3pm-7pm.

physiotherapists
**d. blanjean & m. c. blanjean-
demilt t** 027 771 82 80

police
police cantonale (all crimes) (**c1**) (**t**
027 775 63 20) on Chemin des
Vernes opens Tuesdays, Thursdays
and Saturdays 4:30pm-6pm.
police municipale (**t** 027 77
on Rue de Centre Sportif opens
9:30am-12:15pm and 3pm-6:30pm.

post
The **post office** (**b2**) (**t** 027 771
1044) on Rue de la Poste opens
Monday to Friday 8am-12pm and 2pm-
6pm and Saturday 8am-11am. There is
a 24 hour stamp machine outside.

public holidays

December	6 - St Nicholas Day	
	25 - Christmas Day	
	26 - St Stephen's day	
January	1 - New Year's Day	
March	19 - St Joseph's day	
March/April	Good Friday, Easter Sunday & Monday	

safety on the mountain
avalanche danger - the risk of

directory

avalanche is graded from 1 to 5.
1. (green) low, generally risk-free conditions.
2. (yellow) moderate, favourable conditions for the most part.
3. (dark yellow) considerable, partly infavourable conditions.
4. (orange) high, partly infavourable conditions.
5. (red) very high, skiing not advised. TéléVerbier displays the risk each day at the main lift stations, but if you are in any doubt about where it is safe to ski ask their advice.

food & drink - a skiing holiday is not the time to start a diet. Your body expends energy keeping warm and ⸻ g so it's a good idea to eat a ⸻ breakfast, and carry some ⸻ olate or sweets with you.

⸻ he body dehydrates more quickly at altitude and whilst exercising. You need to drink lots of water each day to replace the moisture you lose.

rules of conduct - the International Ski Federation publishes conduct rules for all skiers and boarders, as summarised.
1. respect - do not endanger or prejudice the safety of others.
2. control - ski in control, adapting speed and manner to ability, the conditions and the traffic.
3. choice of route - the uphill skier must choose his route so he does not endanger skiers ahead.
4. overtaking - allowed above or

below, right or left, but leave enough room for the overtaken skier.
5. entering & starting a run - look up and down the piste when doing so.
6. stopping on the piste - avoid stopping in narrow places or where visibility is restricted.
7. climbing - keep to the side of the piste when climbing up or down.
8. signs & markings - respect these.
9. assistance - every skier must assist at accidents.
10. identification - all involved in an accident (including witnesses) must exchange details.

seasonnaires

in resort - most seasonal workers are English, with some Scandinavians and Antipodeans. The community is fairly friendly although cliques do form among nationalities and companies. One of the more stingy resorts, only the **pub mont fort** offers price reductions for seasonnaires.

jobs - most UK ski companies recruit seasonal workers - interviewing normally starts in May, though there may still be vacancies as late as December. Jobs become available throughout the season, because of staff turnover, illness or accidents. Either contact the companies directly (see **tour operators**), or go through a ski job recruitment website, such as **natives.co.uk** Once employed most companies organise your travel to and from the resort, accommodation, lift pass and equipment rental.

119

directory

work permits - to work legally in Switzerland, you must have a work permit. The rules change on a regular basis - for the 2002/2003 season, the employer applied and purchased the permit for the employee, but it belonged to the employee and allowed them to work anywhere in Switzerland, for any company for the length of its validity. On leaving one company, the employee did not forfeit his permit.

shopping

Most shops open every day (except public holidays) 8:30am-12:30am, and 3pm-7pm.

food

supermarkets - there are six - **primo** (**b2**), **coop** (**a2**), **migros** (**a1**), **PAM** (**a1**), **denner** (**b1**) and the **laterie** (**a4**). Migros only stocks own-brands and does not sell alcohol. Primo on the Place Centrale is the most centrally located but the most expensive. Denner on Rue de Verbier and PAM next to Migros are discount shops so bulk goods or alcohol can be cheaper, whilst the Laterie on Route des Creux is more like a corner shop. On Sundays and some bank holidays, either Primo and Coop or Migros and PAM open - dates and times are posted in their windows.

bread - **michellod** (**c3**) opens at 7:30am to sell fresh bread, pastries, sandwiches, tarts and cakes, as does the bakery (**b/c2**) on Rue de Verbier.

cheese - **la chaumière** (**c2**) on Rue de Médran stocks a mouth-watering selection of international and local cheeses, cured meats and wine. **primo** and **migros** have cheese counters and all the supermarkets sell pre-packed cheese.

chocolate - all the supermarkets (except **migros**) newsagents and newsstands sell the popular Swiss makes - Milka, Lindt, Toblerone. **macbirch** (**d3**) sells individually priced chocolates.

fish - you can buy some fish from **primo, coop** and **migros. le vivier** (**b2**) next to Primo, sells a wider range of fresh and smoked fish as well as some wine and deli products.

meat - **chez camille**, **del maître** and **bruchez frères** all stock a variety of meats and you can also buy rôtisserie chickens - but reserve one in peak weeks - and order a turkey for Christmas. **migros**, **primo** and **coop** have meat counters.

wine & beer - **macbirch** (**b1 & d3**) (**t/f** 027 771 4442) on Rue de Verbier and Rue de Médran stocks local and global wines and spirits and will deliver for free. All the supermarkets, except **migros**, sell wine, beer and spirits.

other

children - **l'igloo** (**e3**) and **le mode des montagnes** (**c2**) for outdoor and

directory

indoor clothing, and **cartoon** (**c2**) and **toy's world** (**c2**) for toys and games.

clothes - **week end** (**e3**) and **degagee** (**d2**) for designer labels, **patagonia** (**e3**) and **quiksilver** (**d3**) for outdoor wear and **soie coquine** (**d2**) for ladies lingerie and swimwear.

florists - **gailland** (**c2**) (**t** 027 771 1717) on Rue de Verbier sells beautiful floral arrangements and will deliver.

gifts - **swiss souvenirs** (**c2**) does what it says on the tin selling cuckoo clocks, stuffed St. Bernard dogs and Swiss Army knifes. **BRV** (**c2**) **l'atelier d'elo** (**b1**) and **yves jacot** (**c1**) sell a selection of watches and jewellery.

ski equipment storage
Lockers are located at Médran (**f4**) - CHF2 for a small locker or ski holder and CHF5 for a big locker. The locker takes your coin as soon as you shut the door, so make sure you have put in/taken out everything you need.

taxis
The tourist office has a full list of taxis in Verbier. The ones below speak decent English.
michaud pascal t 027 771 7196/ 078 721 2121
pierrette coquoz t 027 771 1843/ 079 606 0966 - friendly and reliable
fernades fransisco t 027 771 3465/ 079 220 2088.

telephone
Phones boxes are located by and opposite the post office (**b2**). The minimum cost of any call is 60ct and you can pay by phone card (CHF5/10/20 sold at the post office, and train and petrol stations), credit card or a Swisscom International Prepaid Card (CHF 10/20/50/100). All local and most international calls are cheaper 5pm-8am. The international dialling code for Switzerland is **0041**; the free international operator **0800 801 141**; international direct enquiries **1159**; and national direct enquiries **111**. Swisscom, Sunrise and Orange are the mobile phone networks.

time
Switzerland is always one hour ahead of England.

tipping
Restaurants are obliged by law to work a service charge into the bill, so you don't need to leave a tip.

tour operators
mainstream
airtours t 0870 238 7777
i mytravel.com
crystal t 0870 160 6040
i crystalski.co.uk
first choice t 0870 754 3477
i fcski.co.uk
inghams t 0208 780 4433
i inghams.co.uk
thomson t 0870 888 0254
i thomson-ski.co.uk

directory

specialist
descent t 0207 384 3854
i descent.co.uk
flexiski t 0870 909 0754
i flexiski.com
made to measure t 0124 353 3333
i madetomeasureholidays.com
mountain beds t 0207 924 2650
i mountainbeds.co.uk
simply ski t 0208 541 2209
i simplytravel.co.uk/ski
ski activity t 01738 840 888
i skiactivity.co.uk
ski julia t 0138 658 4478
i skijulia.co.uk
ski total t 0870 163 3633
i skitotal.com
ski world t 0870 241 6723
i skiworld.ltd.uk

verbier specific
peak ski t 01442 832 629
i peak-ski.co.uk
ski armadillo t 07781 411
820/07885 187 293,
i skiarmadillo.com
ski verbier t 0207 385 8050
i skiverbier.com
snowlife t 0124 522 1266
i snowlifechaletholidays.com
sports travel company t 079 584
5490/079 383 0852
i sportstravelcompany.com
vertical reality t 01268 452 337
i verticalrealityverbier.com

weekend specialists
alpine weekends t 0208 944 9762,
i alpineweekends.co.uk
momentum ski t 0207 371 9111
i momentum.uk.com
white roc t 0207 792 1188
i whiteroc.co.uk

tourist information
The tourist office (**c2**) (**t/f** 027 775
3888/3889, **i** verbier.ch) on the Place
Centrale opens Monday to Friday
8:30am-12:30pm and 2pm-6:30pm,
Saturdays 8:30pm-7pm and Sundays
9am-12pm and 4pm-6:30pm. Most
information is free and available in
English.

transport contact numbers
air
bmibaby t 0870 264 2229
i bmibaby.com
british airways t 0870 850 9850
i ba.com
easyjet t 0870 600 0000
i easyjet.co.uk
swiss t 0845 601 0956 **i** swiss.com
geneva airport t 022 717 7111
i gva.ch

coach
alpine express t/f 027 771
9600/9601, **i** alpinexpress.ch
lemania t 027 771 29 55/027 722
5614 **f** 027 722 5610

helicopter
air glaciers t 027 329 1415
i air-glaciers.ch

international train
raileurope t 0870 584 8848
i raileurope.co.uk
eurostar t 0870 518 6186

directory

local bus
post bus t 027 771 1044
i carpostal.ch

local train
rail service t 0900 300 300,
i railaway.ch, cff.ch
le châble t 027 776 1366
martigny t 027 722 4858

tv, video and dvd
swisscom on Rue de la Poste rents
tvs, video and dvd players, videotapes and dvds while **contact
immobilier & video club 7/7** rents
dvds and videotapes.

UK embassy and consulates
uk embassy - Bern **t** 0313 597 700
consulate - Geneva **t** 0227 981 605

water
Tap water is drinkable, except where
there is a eau non potable sign.

wcs
There are public loos at Médran,
Savoleyres and Les Ruinettes.

weather information
Weather and temperature can change
quickly in the mountains. A day which
starts off as clear and sunny can end
in a whirling blizzard. Even in the
resort, air temperature can be very
low and the higher you go up the
mountain, the colder it gets. A strong

wind also lowers the overall
temperature considerably.

weather
i meteosuisse.ch
rhone fm103.3 broadcasts snow
conditions, the weather forecast, and
status of the pistes between 7:30am
and 10:30am in English.

snow and avalanche forecast
infoneige t 027 775 2525
i slf.ch

what to wear
Several, thin layers are better than one
thick piece. Avoid cotton, which keeps
moisture next to the body, so cooling it
down. A strong and wind and moisture
resistant material such as Goretex is
best for outer layers. Gloves and a hat
are also essential.

Always wear sunglasses (or goggles
when cloudy), preferably wrap-around
with shatter-proof lenses giving 100%
protection from UVA and UVB rays. No
or poor eye protection can cause
snowblindness - the eyes water and
feel painful and gritty. Treat by resting
eyes in a darkened room, and applying
cold compresses.

The sun is more intense at high
altitude, so re-apply a high factor SPF
sun protection (from UVA and UVB
rays) regularly, even if overcast and
cloudy and particularly after falling or
sweating. Don't forget ear lobes, and
the underside of the nose.

glossary

a

arête - a sharp ridge.

avalanche - a rapid slide of snow down a slope.

avalanche transceiver - device used when skiing off-piste, which can both emit and track a high frequency signal to allow skiers lost in an avalanche or crevasse to be found.

b

BASI - British Association of Snowsport Instructors.

binding - attaches boot to ski.

black run/piste - difficult, generally steeper than a red piste.

blood wagon - a stretcher on runners used by ski patrollers to carry injured skiers off the mountain.

blue run/piste - easy, generally wide with a gentle slope.

bubble - see '**gondola**'.

button (or Poma) **lift** - for 1 person. Skis and boards run along the ground, whilst you sit on a small 'button' shaped seat.

c

cable car - a large box-shaped lift, running on a thick cable over pylons high above the ground, which carry up to 250 people per car.

carving - a recently developed turning technique used by skiers and boarders to make big, sweeping turns across the piste.

carving skis - shorter and fatter than traditional skis, used for carving turns.

chair lift - like a small and uncomfortable sofa, which scoops you and your skis off the ground and carries you up the mountain. Once on, a protective bar with a rest for your skis holds you in place. Can carry 2-6 people.

couloir - a 'corridor' between two ridges, normally steep and narrow.

crampons - spiked fittings attached to outdoor or ski boots to climb mountains or walk on ice.

d

draglift or (T-bar) - for 2 people. Skis and boards run on the ground, whilst you lean against a small bar.

drop-off - a sharp increase in gradient.

e

edge - the metal ridge on the border of each side of the ski.

f

FIS - Federation Internationale du Ski

flat light - lack of contrast caused by shadow or cloud, making it very difficult to judge depth and distance.

freeriding, **freeskiing** - off-piste skiing.

freestyle - skiing involving jumps.

g

glacier - a slow-moving ice mass formed thousands of years ago and fed each year by fresh snow.

gondola (or bubble) - an enclosed lift, often with seats.

h

heliskiing - off-piste skiing on routes only accessible by helicopter.

high mountain tour (orange) - not groomed, maintained or patrolled, and considered more difficult than all pistes and itinerary routes.

high season - weeks when the

glossary

resort is (generally) at full capacity.

i

itinerary route (yellow) – not groomed, maintained or patrolled. Generally more difficult, at least in part, than a black piste. Can be skied without a guide.

k

kicker - jump.

l

lambchop drag - see '**rope tow**'.

ledgy - off-piste conditions in which there are many short, sharp drop-offs.

low season - beginning and end of the season and the least popular weeks in mid-January.

m

mid season - reasonably popular weeks in which the resort is busy but not full.

mogul - bump, small or large, on or off piste. A large mogulled area is called a mogul field.

o

off-piste - area away from marked, prepared and patrolled pistes.

p

parallel turn - skis turn in parallel.

piste - ski run marked, groomed and patrolled, and graded in terms of difficulty - blue, red or black.

piste basher - bulldozer designed to groom pistes by smoothing snow.

pisteur - ski piste patroller.

Poma - see '**button lift**'.

powder - fresh, unbashed or untracked snow.

r

raquettes - see '**snowshoes**'.

red run/piste - intermediate,

normally steeper than a blue piste, although a flatish piste may be a red because it is narrow, has a steep drop-off or because snow conditions are worse than on other pistes.

rope tow (or lambchop drag) - constantly moving loop of rope with small handles to grab onto to take you up a slope.

s

schuss - a straight slope down which you can ski very fast.

seasonnaire - individual who lives (and usually works) in a ski resort for the season.

skis - technology has changed in the last 10 years. New skis are now shorter and wider. When renting, you will be given a pair approx. 5-10cms shorter than your height.

ski patrol - team of piste patrollers

skins - artificial fur attached to ski base, for ski touring.

snow-chains - chains attached to car tyres so that it can be driven (cautiously) over snow or ice.

snowshoes - footwear resembling tennis rackets which attach to shoes, for walking on soft snow.

spring snow - granular, heavy snow conditions common in late season (when daytime temperatures rise causing snow to thaw and re-freeze).

steeps - a slope with a very steep gradient.

t

T-bar - see '**draglift**'.

w

white-out - complete lack of visibility caused by enveloping cloud cover.

index

index

the authors

Isobel Rostron and Michael Kayson are snowsport enthusiasts who met while taking time out from real life to indulge their passion - Isobel to get it out of her system and Michael to engrain it further. Michael's approach having won, they decided that a return to real life was overrated and came up with a cunning plan to make their passion their work. The result was snowmole.

acknowledgements

None of this would have been possible without the help and support of many people:

Andrew Lilley, Emily Rostron & John Morgan, Angela Horne, Jos Cooke-Priest, Julian Horne, Ali & Nick Smith, Henry & Katie Fyson, Ali Sallaway & Steven Houseman, Tom Fyson, Peter & Christine Rostron, Tom Wedgewood, the boys, Russ Cole, Ben Slatter, Rupert Harbour, Jane Rostron & Tamlyn Stone, Chris Sheedy, Ruff, ginger beer and maltesers and everybody at Cambrian Printers.

accuracy and updates

We have tried our best to ensure that all the information included is accurate at the date of publication. However, because places change - improve, get worse, or even close - you may find things different when you get there. Also, everybody's experience is different and you may not agree with our opinion.

If we learn of any major changes after we have published this guide, we will let you know on our website - www.snowmole.com. You can also help us, in two ways: by letting us know of any changes you notice and by telling us what you think - good or bad - about what we've written. If you have any comments, ideas or suggestions, please write to us at: snowmole, 45 Mysore Road, London, SW11 5RY or send an email to comments@snowmole.com

available from 2004

the snowmole guides to...
• **courchevel les trois vallées**
• **méribel les trois vallées**
• **tignes les trois vallées**
• **val d'isère espace killy**
• **val thorens espace killy**